THE DRY FLY

Progress since Halford

The Dry Fly

Progress since Halford

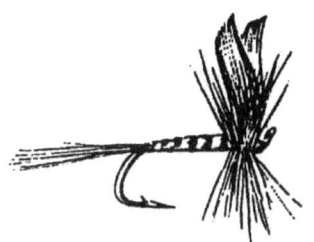

Conrad Voss Bark

Merlin Unwin Books

First published in Great Britain by Merlin Unwin Books Ltd, 1996
This paperback edition published in 2021

All rights reserved
Copyright © the Estate of Conrad Voss Bark

The right of Conrad Voss Bark to be identified as the author of this work has been asserted in accordance with Section 77 of the Copyright, Designs and Patents Act 1988.

All rights reserved, including the right to reproduce this book or portions thereof in any form or by any means, electronic or mechanical, including photocopying, recording, or by any information storage and retrieval system, without permission in writing from the publisher:

Merlin Unwin Books Ltd
Palmers House
7 Corve Street
Ludlow
Shropshire SY8 1DB
U.K.

www.merlinunwin.co.uk

The estate of the author has asserted its moral right to be identified with this work.
ISBN 978-1-913159-32-0
Designed and typeset in Times by Merlin Unwin Books
Printed by Lightning Source

CONTENTS

INTRODUCTION	1
ACKNOWLEDGEMENTS	10
1. THE LOOKING GLASS WORLD	11
2. GHOST WINGS	19
3. THE IMPRESSIONISTS	23
Adams	24
Bi-visible	25
Blue-winged Olive	26
Orange Spinner, David Jacques' BWO,	28
Peter Lapsley's BWO, Parachute Fly,	
Espersen's BWO	31
Caddis Flies - see Sedges and Caddis Flies	31
Caenis	32
Goddard's Last Hope, Skues' Caenis	32
Cul de Canard	33
Daddy Longlegs	34
Funneldun	35
Gold-Ribbed Hare's Ear	38
Winged GRHE & Unwinged GRHE	39
Greenwell	41

Humpy	43
Iron Blue	45
Greene's Iron Blue, Skues' Iron Blue, Houghton Ruby, Dark Watchet	46
Lane's Emerger	49
Leckford Olive Dun	50
Lunn's Olive Dun	51
Lunn's Particular	52
The Big Mayfly	53
Grey Wulff, Shadow Mayfly, Goddard's Poly May Dun and Poly May Spinner, Mick Lunn's Shaving Brush, Alston's Hackle, Black Drake, Fore and Aft Mayfly	54
Microflies: Large Dark Olive, Medium Olive, Blue-winged Olive Dun	62
Midges	65
Midge Emerger, Black Duck Fly, Blagdon Green Midge, Janus, Black Hackle	66
Olive Quill	71
Orange Partridge	72
Parachute Flies	74
Parachute Adams	75
Peacock	76
Pheasant Tail	77
Poult Bloa	78
Red Quill	79
Sedge and Caddis Flies	80
G&H Sedge (Goddard's Caddis), Little Red Sedge, Bighorn Caddis, Caperer, Elk Hair Caddis, Palmer Sedge, Houghton Sedges, Lane's Trimmed Hackle Sedges	80
Sparkle Dun	89

Sparkle Dun	89
Sparkle Spinner	90
Super Grizzly Emerger	91
Terry's Terror	92
Threlfall	93
Upside-Down Flies	94
Wylye Terror	98
4. SIX OF THE BEST	100
Bibliography	107
Appendix: Successful Itchen Flies	109
Index	111

Colour Plates

Plate A
Sparkle Dun, Duck Fly, Blagdon Green Midge, Caperer, Black Gnat,
Beacon Beige, Gold-ribbed Hare's Ear, Micro Orange Quill
USD Dun, Adams, Threlfall, Brown Upright, Houghton Ruby

Plate B
Shadow Mayfly, Alston's Hackle Mayfly
Poly May Dun, Grey Wulff, Poly May Spinner

Plate C
Silver Sedge, Houghton Black Sedge, Terry's Terror
Elk Hair Caddis, Houghton Orange Sedge, Winged Caperer
Little Red Sedge, Humpy, Palmer Sedge, G&H Sedge

Plate D
Winged GRHE, Suspender Midge, Iron Blue Dun
Super Grizzly Emerger, Greenwell's Glory, Lunn's Particular
Leckford Olive Dun, Blue-winged Olive, Lunn's Olive Dun
Dark Watchet, Orange Spinner, Pheasant Tail
Last Hope, Parachute Fly, Funneldun, Janus

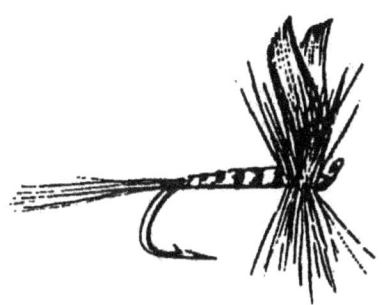

INTRODUCTION

With due deference let us record how much we owe to our ancestors: to begin with, Ogden of Cheltenham and Foster of Ashbourne. They tied the first dry flies, at some time around the 1840s and 50s. Thicker bunches of hackles gave them a longer float than the standard wet fly patterns. Then there was Pulman of Axminster who first called a floating fly a dry fly. He explained that if the trout were taking insects on the surface of the water he 'would take a dry fly' from his box and put it to the trout. The phrase 'dry fly' caught on.

There were many others in the late 1700s and the mid and early 1800s who realised that the trout often took a floating fly before it sank. They made a point of trying to do this: Stewart of Edinburgh, Sir Humphrey Davy, George Bainbridge, Francis Francis, and boys of the Winchester School's fishing society. They whisked the soaked wet flies through the air to dry them before they made a cast.

The first complete description of the dry fly that we have, the design of the flies and the way they should be cast, came from David Foster, the Ashbourne tackle dealer and guide on the Derbyshire Dove. He kept notes of his dry fly system which were not dated but were probably written between the 1840s and 60s or early 70s. They were edited posthumously by his sons and published in 1882 as *The Scientific Angler*. There, precise in every detail, was the dry fly as we know it.

The wet flies of that time had very little hackle because the hackle was supposed to represent the legs of the insect. Foster didn't accept this. He made his hackle 'ample and full to assist

David Foster, the first to define the dry fly as we now know it

Introduction

flotation'. He goes on:

> ...with the duns the wings must be full and erect, or 'cock up' as it is sometimes designated, so as to admit the fly [with the full hackle] to be comparatively dry for some little time, when, becoming saturated, a few backwards and forwards whisks of the line and rod should be given before the next cast again. This is repeated whenever the flies become saturated as by so doing the trouble of repeatedly changing the lure is greatly lessened.

That last sentence is his reply to Pulman of Axminster who, in his book *The Vade Mecum of Fly Fishing for Trout* (1841), recommended changing the soaked fly for a dry one when the trout were feeding on the surface. A fly that would float much longer without being changed was Foster's answer. He goes on to say

> The dry fly system is... by far the most scientific and artistic way of alluring trout or grayling, and well-fished streams will yield more and heavier dishes of fish to it than any other method or system of angling whatever.

But the most remarkable thing about Foster which has been overlooked by other writers, such as Waller Hills, is that he emphasises that the artificial fly must be regarded from below rather than looking down on it from above when the fly is being designed and tied. In this he was far in advance of the views of Halford and Marryat who only tried to get close imitations of the natural insect and never considered looking at their flies from below, from the trout's point of view.

One cannot help wondering why Halford and Marryat did not pay tribute to Foster for his work on the dry fly. When Foster's book was published Halford and Marryat were carrying out their own researches on the Test. Foster's book was reviewed in the angling journals and would have been in the library of the Flyfishers' Club

Frederic M. Halford, who established his famous dry fly code

of which Halford was a member.

It was curious that Halford never mentioned Foster. There may have been many reasons; he was too busy, he hadn't heard of Foster's book, it was not written by Foster but by his sons, they may have exaggerated their father's theories. It could have been any of these reasons.

Halford's first book, *Floating Flies and Flow to Dress Them,* was published in 1886, four years after Foster's. It was a remarkable book in every way and rightly praised. It insisted

INTRODUCTION

upon a rigid discipline and the closest possible imitation of the natural insect, even to the colour of its eyes. All his flies - there were a hundred dressings - were designed to float, and on the whole they floated better than any previous patterns. They can still be seen in the library of The Flyfisher's Club, beautiful little things, and how important were the delicate bodies, made of quill to help flotation.

Halford's relationship with Marryat was, to begin with, that of a pupil to a teacher. He met Marryat by chance in 1879 and was at once aware of Marryat's greater knowledge about flies and fishing. Marryat was once described by Edward Grey, later Viscount Grey of Fallodon, as being 'the best trout fisherman in England'. Marryat was a retired Indian Army Officer who spent most of his time fishing the Test. Halford frequently went to him for advice. They became friendly.

In 1880 Halford took rooms at Bossington Mill at the end of the Houghton Club water of the Test, with the intention of studying the river flies and their matching artificials. He asked Marryat to join him and after six years' intensive work by them both, Halford's first book was published. He asked Marryat to be co-author as Marryat had in fact done a very large part of their research but Marryat refused. No one knew why he refused and Marryat himself never said. They merely parted and there was no explanation.

They had been together in close company for six years and over such a time they had got to know each other well and it has always seemed to me that Marryat gradually began to dislike Halford's dictatorial attitude to the dry fly. As Waller Hills remarked in his *A History of Fishing for Trout:*

> ...[Halford] considered that the dry fly had superseded for all time and in all places all other methods of fly fishing and that those who thought otherwise were either ignorant or incompetent.

The Dry Fly

We know that Marryat did not take that attitude. A fly box of his which I once saw in the library of The Flyfishers' Club contained the kind of wet flies that Skues would have used before he tied his nymph patterns. In other words, Marryat liked to fish the dry fly but he was no purist and would fish a wet fly from time to time if conditions demanded it, if the trout were feeding under water on the ascending nymphs.

Halford was becoming an ultra purist; that is, he would not put a fly to a rising trout until he was certain that the trout was feeding on the hatching duns. This was one reason why he gave up using the Gold-Ribbed Hare's Ear which he suspected was being taken as a hatching nymph. In other words, as someone said, the hare's ear wasn't dry enough.

It was inevitable that during their work capturing insects in the river, mounting them, copying them, discussing their behaviour and experimenting with various dressings, they would get to know each other's nature and it must have been clear to both of them that they were drifting apart. Halford did the right thing in asking Marryat to be the joint author of *Floating Flies* and Marryat, aware of Halford's growing intolerance, politely declined. Marryat was never a critic of Halford. He remained silent.

So Halford has all the praise for the Red and Blue and Ginger Quills, the Grannom, the Black Gnat, the Silver Sedges, the Alder and all the rest of these remarkable flies which are so beautifully designed and tied. Moreover, his tactics were extremely sound. He even suggested that there were times when the dry fly could be drifted downstream to a rising trout if it could not be reached in any other way - a tactic that is now widely forgotten by the ultra purists of Halford's followers.

Halford was the great publicist of the dry fly. Waller Hills, who was highly critical of Halford's authoritarian views, which we've just quoted, nevertheless has written the best summary of Halford's influence and achievement:

INTRODUCTION

> ...two tendencies are apparent. The floating fly has spread far beyond its original territory. When he first wrote, it was the common but not yet the universal practice in a limited area: the chalkstreams of Hampshire, Berkshire, Wiltshire and Kent, the Wandle, Hertfordshire and Buckingham streams, and the limestone streams of Derbyshire. Speaking generally (and without reckoning such outlying areas such as the Driffield Beck) Derbyshire was its northerly and Dorsetshire its westerly boundary. At his death [in 1914] it had spread over all England, over Scotland, Ireland, parts of France, Germany, Scandinavia, America and New Zealand, in fact it was practised by some fishermen in most places where trout are to be found. It must not be imagined that wherever it went it conquered for that was far from the case. But it won its way on rivers where trout sometimes run large, such as Tweed or Don, and particularly on Irish rivers of which the Suir is one. It has also come to be used more and more on lakes which hold big fish, such as Blagdon or Lough Arrow. And the new sport of fishing it for sea trout has been invented. Altogether, Halford, in the time between his first book and his death [1886–1914] saw its empire spread over a large part of the earth.

True enough. All the same, many men were fishing the dry fly or 'the floater' years before Halford, who had begun his fishing life as a coarse angler. A friend took him to the Wandle where he was advised by members of the syndicate there to fish the dry fly upstream to rising fish, a technique known at the time as 'the Carshalton dodge'.

Ten years before that, Francis Francis had been enthusiastically commending the dry fly in articles in *The Field*. Halford was caught up in a growing tide of enthusiasm for the dry fly, improved upon it with Marryat's help and eventually led it in the direction we now know. It was indeed a great achievement to establish the dry fly code and to publicise it in those remarkable six books of his but the general movement of opinion towards the dry fly by many fishermen began while Halford was still at school. To say this is not to denigrate his achievement as the historian and publicist of the dry fly but to put it in perspective.

Although Marryat's and Halford's patterns of the new dry flies were infinitely more lifelike to look at than those that had been in use before, many efforts were made to improve upon them. First was Dr J.C. Mottram who was a most inventive fly designer, pioneering dressings that created the illusion of the natural insect, its silhouette against the light.

He also produced midge pupae with cork bodies and an olive spinner with a bare hook abdomen. His book, *Fly Fishing, Some New Arts and Mysteries*, was published by *The Field*, undated, probably in 1915 or 16 during the First World War. It was not the most appropriate moment to produce a largely technical book when most of its potential readers were involved in France and Flanders. Moreover his flies looked a little odd.

Ten years later an aeronautical engineer, J.W. Dunne, who was also searching for the translucent appearance of the dun's body and wings, painted the shanks of his hooks white and used a kind of rayon floss (cellulite) which became almost transparent when oiled and wet. It worked well but unfortunately the necessary material, cellulite, went out of production. There were other experiments but the tremendous scope of Halford's books, the precision and clarity of his description of how to fish the dry fly, could never be challenged. This is classic Halford:

> Dry fly fishing is presenting to the rising fish the best possible imitation of the insect on which he is feeding in its natural position. To analyse this further, it is necessary, firstly, to find a fish feeding on the winged insect; secondly, to present to him a good imitation of this insect, both as to size and colour; thirdly, to present it to him in its natural position floating on the surface of the water with its wings

Introduction

up, or what we technically term 'cocked'; fourthly, to put the fly lightly on the water so that it floats accurately over him without drag; and fifthly to take care that all these conditions have been fulfilled before the fish has seen the angler or the reflection of his rod.

It is a splendid description of how to fish the dry fly but it misses the crucial point about the fly itself: what does the artificial look like to the trout who sees it not from above but from under the surface of the water?

I suspect that both Marryat and Halford were aware that the trout might find its observation distorted by the water to some extent but they thought that if they made the closest possible copy of the natural insect this would be sufficient to deceive the trout. What they didn't realise, but Foster suspected, is that the trout saw *both* the artificial and the natural fly in strange ways which neither Halford nor Marryat imagined possible.

The mistake was realised some 20 or so years after Halford's death. Efforts were then made to design new patterns of the dry fly not as seen from above through the air but as the trout sees them looking up through the distorting element of water.

That is the theme of this book, this revolutionary change in our attitude to the dry fly.

Conrad Voss Bark
Lifton, Devon. May 1996

Acknowledgments

I am most grateful to Nick Lyons for permission to use Vincent Marinaro's photograph on page 18 and to John Goddard for those on pages 20 and 21. In addition, I must thank both John Goddard and Peter Deane for the flies they tied for me which form the bulk of the illustrations.

I would also like to thank many individual fishermen who have helped with information and replies to my enquiries about flies and fly designs. They include George Aitken, J. Adamson, Robert H. Berls, John Betts, W. E. Bisland, Nick Brabner, Anthony Bridgett, Jack Burke, Hugh Clarke, Lt. Col. D. D. Campbell, Roy Darlington, Geoffrey Dashwood, the Bolton Abbey Estate, Peter Deane, Joe Devine, Donald Downs, Morgens Espersen, John Goddard, Dr Godfrey Herrington, Ron Holloway, Steven Kemp, Nick Lyons, Mick Lunn, Pat O'Reilly, Peter O'Reilly, Neil Patterson, Major Hugh Pollen, Gordon Mackie, Craig Mathews, E.J.T. Matthews, J. Reid, Kenneth Robson, Guy Robinson, Robert Starr, Tom Valentine, A. Willis, Colton P. Wagner and Herb Wellington.

I have also been fortunate as a member of the Flyfishers' Club in London having access to their extensive library. A list of the main books that have been of use will be found in the Bibliography on pages 106 and 107. I would also like to thank many of my American friends, some whose names are unknown to me, for their streamside conversations and advice.

To my dear wife Anne my deepest gratitude for her constant encouragement and support.

---— **Footnotes** ———

The footnotes can be found, listed in numerical sequence, at the end of each chapter in which they occur.

1. THE LOOKING GLASS WORLD

Some day anglers will learn to combine a judicious admixture of wet fly science and dry fly art, and then - then will be the time for new development.

G.E.M. Skues, *The Fly Fishers' Journal*, Spring, 1931

Fishing with Skues on the Abbotts Barton Water of the Itchen in the 1920s was a pensioner from the 1914–18 war, an officer of the Marines, Colonel E.W. Harding. We know little about him except that a book of his was published in 1931 - *The Flyfisher and the Trout's Point of View* - which was largely ignored by the dry fly fishermen of the chalkstreams at the time but which has had a most significant part to play in the design of the dry fly since Halford.

Harding set up an observation tank at his home at Iwerne Courtney, near Blandford, in Dorset, filled it with water, and from a glass peephole at one side would watch flies, real ones and artificials, floating on the surface.

To his suiprise, a large part of the water surface was opaque, acting as a mirror that reflected the bottom of the tank. Flies floating on the surface of this mirror area could not be seen as flies at all, only the imprints or light patterns they made on the surface which looked like pits, small indentations, little blobs, which were caused by the hackles or bodies of the flies which supported them on the water. The fly itself could not be seen.

Even more strange were the curious sparkles of light which surrounded these imprints from the feet or hackle of the dun, light patterns which varied according to the shape and size of the indentations on the water.

Harding was bewildered by what he saw. He told Skues about it and Skues urged him to make a serious study of the subject and to publish the findings. Whether Skues came to Iwerne Courtney to see these mysterious imprints and sparkles of light for himself we do not know. There is no record of it but all one can say is that it was most likely. He was very enthusiastic about Harding's discoveries as we know from his books.

So Harding set to work, making notes of what he saw. The more he explored this underwater world the more surprising, indeed bewildering, he found it. It was something like Lewis Carroll's looking glass world and in *Alice in Wonderland* where everything became 'curiouser and curiouser' the more Alice explored it.

Even more curious was what happened when the fly floated out of the mirror area into another area where the trout could see a distorted picture of the world outside. This was called the trout's window - a window on the world - but ripples on the water made the world look very queer and shaky. Moreover the size of the trout's window, a circular area, altered with the position of the trout in the water. If the trout was low down near the bottom, the circular window was quite large, but this diminished the closer the trout got to the surface. Finally, it would disappear as the trout broke the surface.

Even more peculiar, as the winged fly approached the window and the trout was rising towards it, the wings of the fly appeared to leave the body of the fly, detaching themselves from it and hovering above it. An illusion of course, but real enough to the trout:

> Only when the fly got near the centre of the window, [said Harding] would it appear as a natural fly more or less as we see them, and not blobs of shadow surrounded by haloes of light. By then, the trout, if rising to the take, would be so close to the surface that the window would be broken by the ripples of the bulge of water coming from below caused by the rising bulk of the fish...[and]...it is only when the fly is well in the centre of the window, providing the fish keeps sufficiently below the surface and the light comes from behind it, that the colour of the fly becomes important...[so from what is seen of the fly in the mirror and the window]... it is not difficult to lay down a specification for the floating dun from these data. And that specification is something entirely different from any idea of exact imitation.

He described the different light patterns of the natural insects:

> The dun makes one pattern of sparkles and the spent spinner with its body possibly in the surface film and held up by its outstretched wings, makes another. The newly hatched dun, while resting on its shuck as a raft, would make yet another; while the sparkles from the nymph in the act of hatching and those from the sedge scuttling over the surface of the water differ from each other and from those of the dun and spinner.

The Dry Fly

On the subject of the trout's eyesight, the trout's eyes are more or less structured in the same way as the human. Harding quotes a fishery biologist, Dr Ward, saying we shall not be very far wrong in assuming that the trout sees objects under water in very much the same way as we do. What we cannot say is what the trout thinks it sees. However, 'centuries of angling practice proves that this does not matter.'

Taking the same line as his friend G.E.M. Skues, Harding said it did not matter much from the trout's point of view whether one fished a wet fly or a dry.

Harding's description of what the trout can see of the floating fly occupies a comparatively small number of the book's 200 pages. One can summarise most of the rest.

Taking his favourite fly, the Greenwell, he suggests ways in which it could be tied to suggest a number of duns instead of one particular insect, say a medium olive. The quality of the Greenwell's head hackle is what matters. There should be three or at the most four turns of the best quality cock hackle, tied in very close turns, each turn being pressed close to the previous one so that the fibres radiating, as it were, from a tiny area of the hook shank, will produce the little group of sparkling points which is the light pattern of the floating dun.

Tied correctly, the Greenwell could be regarded as representing a range of duns extending from the large dark olive at one end to the darker pale wateries at the other.

He was one of the first to suggest that the nymph, emerging on the surface of the water, was a legitimate form of the dry fly, and said that the Gold-Ribbed Hare's Ear was a typical example of an emerger.

The Skues dressing of the Little Red Sedge was a standard dressing that would, with suitable variations of size, represent every kind of sedge fly.

Harding went on to discuss many subjects: refraction, the entry of light into the water, illustrated with a number of complex drawings; different rise forms; casting and striking; hooks; lines; rods; and flyfishing literature.

The book was not well received. Chalkstream fishermen resented criticism of the dry fly code and of Halford. Moreover the book itself did not help. The diagrams were obscure and the watercolour illustrations amateurish. There were bad reviews and the book seemed to be generally regarded as the work of a crank. Harding died not long after publication, but so far as I can tell he was aware that the book had at least been well received in the United States.

One of America's leading flyfishermen, Vincent Marinaro, had been experimenting along the same lines as Harding and was enthusiastic. Some years later, he used a quotation from Harding in the opening chapter of his best-selling book, *A Modern Dry Fly Code*, and was able to summarise Harding's main thesis with considerable precision.

Strict imitation of the natural fly was not possible:

> It cannot be done in the way of Halford, Ronalds, and others of ancient fame, for they spoke of imitation in terms of human vision and comprehension supported only by the prop of entomology. That way alone lies grave error, since it does not take into account the vision of the trout and the geometry of the underwater world: and the study of entomology stops short, far short, of the approaches to these considerations, which are the dominant factors in devising imitations.

Marinaro carried out many experiments, finally producing a dry fly which he called the Thorax Dun. Admirable when correctly tied but to tie it was time-consuming, difficult, and so far as the trade was concerned, uneconomic.

However, the idea of a fly that was simple and easy to tie which gave the right impression to the trout was an idea that began to spread. To say that it was all due to the unknown retired Marine

THE DRY FLY

Vincent Marinaro, inventor of the Thorax Dun

and his water tank at Iwerne Courtney would be wrong but he had played his part; and it was an important part, not only in the United States but here in Britain, firstly among a small group of enthusiasts on the Hungerford water of the Kennet. But that is a story I shall tell when we come to the mayfly.

The search for the new dry flies was not a search for the infallible fly, only for a fly that, if properly presented, would suggest the possibility to the fish that what he sees is likely to be worth eating. Infallibility does not arise in such a context because of the imponderables of chance, the effects of wind and water, light and sunshine, cloud and shadow, of the way the fly falls and where it falls, of how it drifts and how it looks. So many things are involved that there always seems to be an element of magic about a sudden unexpected rise and take. The fly itself, the impression of a fly, is both a part and at the same time the centre of this mysterious process:

> The fly is the historical constant, and the entire evolution of fly fishing equipment, techniques and practices has been only a series of changes to improve the way we manage this unchanging fact. But the fly is an end as well as a beginning. It forms the terminus of all our preparations, study, practice and observation. Once it is freely drifting on the current the matter is pretty much out of our hands. We've done all we can to make the fly and its behaviour convincing, and now consolidate desire, anticipation and hope into this bit of floating fluff. The rest is up to the trout.
>
> (Ted Leeson, *The Habit of Rivers*)

But what we now have to accept is that what the trout sees of the fly is not what we think it sees. We now know that the trout lives in what is to us a completely bewildering world in which the trout does not see a delicate little fly but a sequence of sparkling blobs.

The camera of John Goddard in this country and of Vince Marinaro in the United States have brought this home to us. Marinaro speculated in the 1950s after reading Harding that 'we cannot afford to be dogmatic' about what the trout sees of the fly. We now know, he went on, much of the nature of a trout's eyesight and of the peculiar physical laws which affect what the trout sees. However, it was not until Marinaro began using an underwater camera that the evidence was first published. Here it is, from Marinaro's *In the Ring of the Rise*: the looking glass world of the trout.

The artificial dry fly (left) and the natural fly seen from underwater: a photograph taken by Vincent Marinaro and published in his book In the Ring of the Rise in 1976.

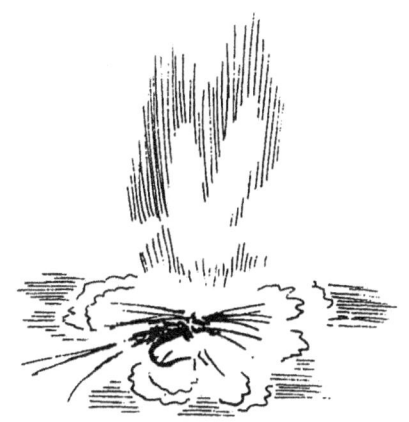

2. Ghost Wings

Lovers, poets, religious madmen and anglers seem to me to have this in common - they live for the impassioned anticipation of an uncertain thing.

Ted Leeson, *The Habit of Rivers*

For each generation there are new flies. They come and go, about every century, into and out of fashion. Some of the greatest survive by adaptation, the Hare's Fleck becoming the Hare's Ear, but mostly they seem to die with the death of those who have been in love with them, which is sad but is the way of the world.

The Dry Fly

John Goddard, pioneer of the new dry flies

The new flies have been and are continuing to be developed in attempts to meet the new knowledge of the trout's world that was not available to our grandfathers or in many cases our fathers.

There will also be flies for the coming century, to be tested against a community of experience on a multitude of rivers against a background of greater knowledge. The search for perfection is endless and inevitable, always coinciding with the knowledge that it can never be reached. All the same it is best to travel hopefully with our illusions, however unlikely and illogical they may be.

Even so, the work of Harding and those who followed him, both in England and in many parts of the United States, has meant that we have made what might well be called a modicum of progress in the design of our dry flies. We no longer feel it

Ghost Wings

necessary, as Halford did, to imitate the colour of an insect's eye by an appropriate turn of the right-coloured silk between the head hackle and the eye of a hook. Close or exact imitation is not necessarily what we attempt to achieve now.

We think instead of imprints on the trout's mirror made by the feet of a dun or the wings and body of a spinner, and we attempt to give the impression of these rather than make reasonable models of a fly as we see it in the hand. Indeed we have largely given up modelling flies, in the knowledge that the trout will not be impressed with what he is unable to see because of his existence in the peculiar geometry of the underwater world.

One of the strangest effects of this strange world is what Harding called 'the flare' of a fly's wings which appear to leave the body of the fly as it approaches the rim of the trout's window. It was not easily believed by the chalkstream fishermen of the 1930s, and indeed this was one of the reasons why Harding was thought of as a crank, or at best mistaken. It was really too difficult to imagine that wings could leave the body of a fly, hover above it, then sink back

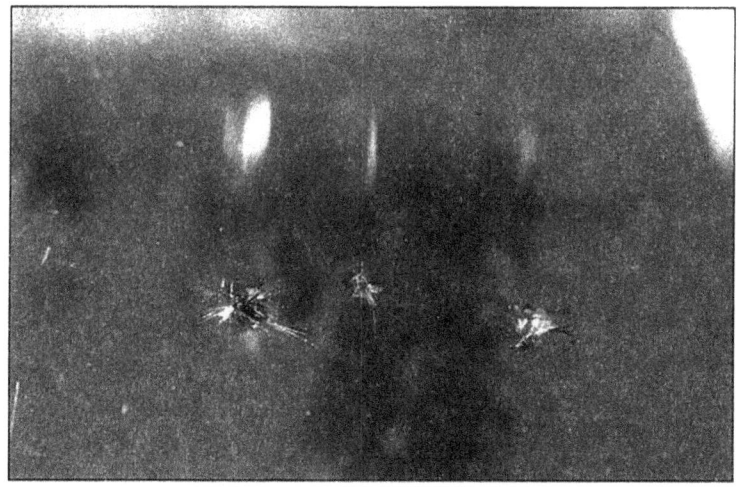

Goddard and Clarke's evidence of the 'ghost wings'

and be reunited with a body which had appeared to have no wings at all. Curiouser and curiouser, as Harding said.

But snorkelling and underwater cameras have since confirmed that the impossible does take place. The evidence is overwhelming. Dedicated work over many years by two flyfishermen, John Goddard and Brian Clarke, on the Wilderness water of the Kennet, produced the evidence in an important book, *The Trout and the Fly, a New Approach*. Goddard's underwater camera showed clearly the so-called 'ghost wing' effect of the wings of a dun leaving the body.

Goddard was able to photograph the fly (see page 21) as it came closer to the rim of the window until the wings gradually got nearer to the body of the fly. This showed the importance of the wings as 'the second trigger in the predatory mechanism of the trout'[1].

The first trigger was when the trout saw the imprints of the fly in the mirror. That alerted the trout to the possibility of food so that he would rise to meet the fly floating down to the window. An experienced trout might wait and examine it more closely, following the fly downstream.

So now we move towards a new century armed with a new theory of the design of the dry fly. We have left the Victorians behind.

Footnote

1. Reproduced by kind permission of John Goddard and Ernest Benn Ltd from *The Trout and the Fly* (1980)

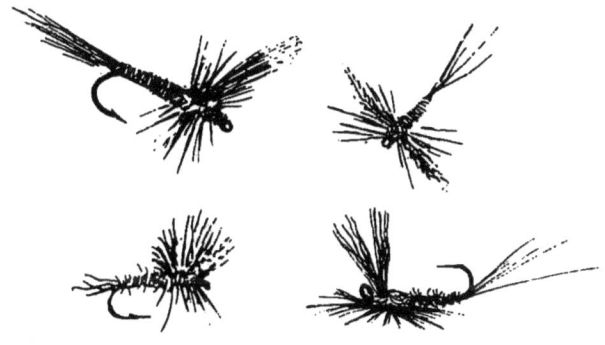

3. THE IMPRESSIONISTS

The following list includes three different types of fly. First, the new designs based on the Harding formula, or a similar formula, which is not concerned with making a copy or a model of an insect but creating a fly, which we have called an impressionist fly, which gives the right imprint and light pattern to the trout.

Secondly, it includes those traditional flies which over many years, in several cases more than a hundred years, have by chance succeeded in making the right impression on the trout even though they were originally tied as copies or models of an insect.

Thirdly, it includes several North Country wet fly patterns which can also be fished dry or as emergers, particularly to suggest many of the Baetis spinners.

A test of the value of the new impressionist flies, whatever their origin, is whether they can in general successfully represent groups of insects rather than an individual member of a group.

THE DRY FLY

THE ADAMS

The most popular, and the best-selling fly in America, according to Paul Schullery,[1*] the Adams is also by far and away the most effective of all the flies used on the Abbotts Barton water of the Itchen.[2]

Of the many tributes to the Adams, in Britain and in the States, that of Poul Jorgensen sums it up admirably: 'It does not represent anything in particular but can be fished anywhere successfully all the the year round'.[3]

The Adams makes a good imprint and light pattern on the water. It has good ghost wings. The hook is lifted clear of the water by an exceptionally long tail, which in practice is one of several important features of the design.

It is one of the high-riding flies that are becoming more and more popular among perceptive American flydressers, making the imprints on the water only by the hackle and tail. Nothing else.

The design was developed in 1922 by Leonard Halliday of Mayfield, Michigan. A friend of his, Charles F. Adams, an attorney from Ohio, was the first to use it and was so enthusiastic that Halliday named the fly after him. Some of the Adams seen in the shops in Britain have little relationship with the original, generally lacking the length and strength of the tail.

---

*Footnotes are to be found at the end of the chapter

The dressing, which I believe is close to the original, is as follows:

Hook: 10 or 12 to 18 depending on the size of the natural flies on the water.
Wings: two grizzle hackle tips, upright and a little spread, not too close to the head of the hook.
Tail: a number of long mixed grizzly and brown hackles tied close together. Alternatively, a long thin hackle point serves well as it is stiffer than the bunch of fibres and helps lift, the hook clear of the water.
Body: muskrat.
Front hackle: mixed brown and grizzly.

Other variations include a dressing that leaves out the wings and another which ties in the wings almost spent to suggest the spinner, the imago. You can also use synthetics for the tail and rabbit or hare's fur for the body, ribbed with fine wire.

The Adams suggests practically all the mayflies, olives, iron blues, blue-winged olives and pale wateries.

BI-VISIBLE

No one quite knows the origin of the Bi-visible. It is similar in a way to the Loch Ordie, a salmon fly. It was a favourite for trout with Ed Hewitt on the Neversink River in the States, where, he said, it would often bring up a trout when there was no hatch. It must be older then either of those for the palmer dressing, of which this is a variant, goes back as far as the Middle Ages; so it joins the traditional flies that also make a good light pattern.

You can use the Bi-visible for so many things. It is an ideal top dropper for fishing the drift on Irish and Scottish lochs. It can suggest hawthorn flies when there is a good fall of those, it is an excellent black gnat and reed smut, the hackles give a good imprint of a Baetis, while at a pinch it can stand in for a Shadow Mayfly.

Hook: as small as 18 and as large as 10.
Hackle: black cock, palmered from head to bend of the hook. Two turns of a white hackle at the head are useful for seeing the fly on the water and possibly suggesting wings.

If you leave out the white hackle then the fly is known as a Black Hackle and stands in for most of the things a Bi-visible does. For Midges see page 65.

BLUE-WINGED OLIVE

Mainly a fly of the chalkstreams, hatching in the dusk and the darkness, the blue-winged olive has confused generations of fishermen who have been so confident that they know how to cope with the enigma of the evening rise. Legends abound: that

The Impressionists

Guy Robinson, advocate of the Orange Spinner during BWO rises

the trout rises with a kidney-shaped boil; that it does not rise with a kidneyshaped boil; that it has a fascination for the Orange Quill; that it does not have a fascination for the Orange Quill.

One of the problems is that there are times when the spinner is on the water at about the same time as the dun. There are two good patterns of the spinner, the Pheasant Tail and the Orange Spinner, the latter being the momentary favourite. 'Always try the Orange Spinner,' says Guy Robinson, water keeper at Leckford on the Test, 'at the start of the blue-winged olive rise.'

THE DRY FLY

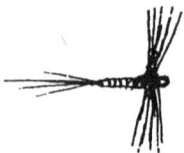

ORANGE SPINNER

Hook: 14 or 16.
Tying silk: plain orange.
Whisks: four long strands of honey dun cock spade hackle; or microfibetts.
Body: medium orange fur ribbed with fine gold wire.
Hackle: rusty dun cock tied at right angles to hook shank.

A modern dressing makes good use of synthetics:

Hook: 14 or 16.
Tying silk: plain orange.
Body: medium orange synthetic fur ribbed fine gold wire.
Wings: white sparkle polypropolene yarn tied at right angles to the hook shank.
Body: dubbing could be Antron mixed with hare's ear. The wing should not be bunched tightly. There should be light between the fibres.

David Jacques who fished at Marsh Court below Stockbridge for many years made a special study of the blue-winged olive dun and spinner.[1] He came to the conclusion that the orange bodied artificial is accepted by the trout only when spinners are on the water and rejected decisively when they are not. Jacques copied the dun closely:

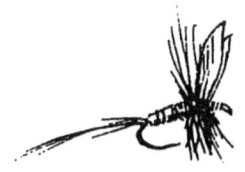

DAVID JACQUES' BWO

Hook: 14.
Tying silk: hot orange.
Hackle and whisks: dirty dark orange cock.
Body: green plastic over yellow ostrich herl.
Wings: two pairs from the wing feather of a coot.

You may have problems getting green plastic. Jacques used picric acid to dye the plastic but this is now on the reserved list. It should not be too difficult to get a greeny yellow dubbing. Variations of the original dressing are still seen at Marsh Court.

A later version of the blue-winged olive comes from Peter Lapsley. It would do quite well as an emerger.

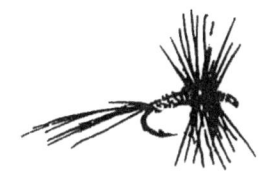

Peter Lapsley's BLUE-WINGED OLIVE

Hook: 14.
Tail: pale blue dun cock.
Body: yellow tying silk lightly dubbed with a 50/50 mix of olive and brown fur.

Head hackle: blue dun and reddish brown cock hackle wound together.

You might try cutting a V in the hackle to allow the body to come closer to the surface of the water to suggest the dun emerging from the nymph and if you do this then outrigger synthetic fibres might support the fly better than the pale blue dun.

THE PARACHUTE FLY

A new development has been the use of the parachute fly for the blue-winged olive during the evening rise. Good reports of its effectiveness have come in from the Itchen, the Test at Chilbolton, and the Kennet at Hungerford.

An impressive dressing comes from Morgens Espersen of Denmark. He says that on Danish rivers the blue-winged olive hatches from early June until very late in the autumn. It has an olive body early in the season which gradually becomes reddish brown later on. He changes the colour of the artificial's body as the season progresses.

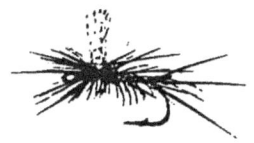

Espersen's Blue-Winged Olive

Hook: 14-16, Mustad 94840.
Thread: tan colour, very thin (Unithread 8/0 or Sparton Midge).
Tail: three hairs from a brown nylon paintbrush, tied split (outrigger style).
Body: Fly-rite dubbing, colour according to season.
Wing spike: smoke-grey poly yarn.
Hackle: medium brown cock wound parachute style round the base of the wing.

According to the latest information about the evening rise it is probably best to see if there are spinners on the water to begin with and if there is no response then presumably the dun will work. But the evening rise is so unpredictable that such a sequence may not always be correct.

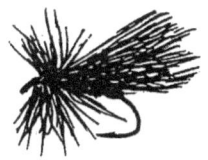

Caddis Flies

This is where we come up against the naming of flies. American anglers, sensibly, call the caddis fly the 'caddis fly' because it hatches from the caddis grub.

The English call the caddis fly a 'sedge fly'. The reason dates back to somewhere prior to 1000 AD, when the Old English word 'secg' was used by our ancestors to describe flies of unknown origin which were generally found flying close to the sedge that grew by the banks of rivers and lakes.

Tradition, sentiment and common usage are difficult to ignore. Caddis flies are included with sedge flies on page 80.

CAENIS

A tiny little mayfly. Sometimes lakes and rivers have enormous hatches. Frank Sawyer, describing a hatch on the Upper Avon, said that 'both sexes dance and weave with the vagaries of air currents about ten or twelve feet above the water looking at a distance as much the same as a cloud of gnats on a summer evening... the duns hatch in such numbers that there are times when the river boils with fish.'[4]

GODDARD'S LAST HOPE

The latest pattern to suggest the Caenis and a good one.

Hook: 18.
Tying silk: yellow.

Body: grey or cream Norwegian goose primary herls.
Hackle: cream or light honey cock very short in the flue.
Tails: 6 to 8 nylon microfibetts.

Skues' Caenis

The following is a simplification of the Skues dressing to suggest both dun and spinner.

Hook: 18.
Tail: a few strands of white hackle..
Body: white or pale cream silk.
Head hackle: small white cock hackle with V cut underneath so that the fly rests close to the water.

Cul de Canard

In English it would be called a Duck's Bottom Fly as the soft whiskery hackle comes from the preen gland of a duck which is close to its bottom. These hackles are said to be waterproof but not I think in the sense in which elk or deer hair is waterproof. One cannot get over the impression that it is a novelty which is liked by flydressers and tackle shops as it is so simple, quick and easy to tie and can be sold with many names such as a 'Blue-Winged Olive

C de C' and so on. The hackle has the same appearance as grey polypropylene. Its use for dry flies may be limited to the wings of spinners or possibly an emerger dun, but for either purpose they would be found rather soft.

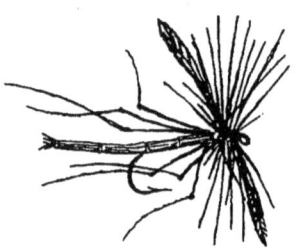

DADDY LONGLEGS

A crane fly, a terrestrial, which hatches in mid-summer. The daddy longlegs is mainly of interest to lake fishermen as it is a poor flyer and in a high wind gets blown over the borders of lakes in quite large numbers. Many years ago at Weir Wood there were dozens on the water all fluttering their wings and legs and the trout were lining up with slashing takes.

River trout seem to be a little nervous of them, often bashing at the fluttering insect with their tails, drowning it, and then taking it. This happens irregularly. On the big natural lakes of Scotland and Ireland an artificial Daddy is sometimes fished as a top fly on a drift, as often as not when there are no natural flies to be seen.

> **Hook:** 10 or 12.
> **Body:** half a dozen fibres from the tail of a cock pheasant, glued together, whipped with brown thread, projecting beyond the bend of the hook.
> **Legs:** half a dozen cock pheasant fibres, knotted in the middle, tied in raggedly.

The Impressionists

Wings: two quite large hackle points, grizzly, pale dun or honey dun, tied in at right angles to the body.

The Funneldun

A most interesting and ingenious fly which was designed by Neil Patterson to represent a great number of different kinds of insects. It is, he says, a design for the medium and small dry flies whether they are olives, gnats, hawthorns, midge, or even sedge. It is a claim which is explained and described fully in a new book of his which has just been published.[5]

Patterson says that he set out to correct four basic design faults of traditional dry flies. First, they needed very high quality and expensive cock hackles. Secondly, he believed that the traditional mounting of the hackles at right angles to the hook shank actually encourages the fly to sink. Third, that in the trout's window the thorax of the natural insect - clearly visible from the advantage of an underwater tank - is absent on the traditional dryfly. Lastly, the traditional fly floats down the stream the wrong way up, exposing the sight of the hook to the trout.

Neil Patterson: seeking a fly that always lands hook up

It was while experimenting with low grade hackles that the idea came to him to 'funnel' them over the eye of the hook so that the fly rested not on the points of the hackles, as with conventional flies, but on the flattened edge of the hackles.

He emphasises that the Funneldun is an improved design - a system of tying dry flies and not a pattern or an imitation of any one natural fly in particular. He uses small up-eyed hooks, small for a good reason. The forward-sloping hackles protrude slightly in front of the fly. This makes the Funneldun fly a little longer than if it was tied by the conventional method. So, if he wants a size 14 fly he ties in a size 16, and for a 16 fly he ties in an 18.

> 'This is a bonus. It means the hook is smaller and lighter in proportion to the fly size. With less iron to hunk around Funneldums float like balsa wood. And I don't add ribbing as extra cargo.'

This is the dressing:

A light fur is dubbed on to the tying thread and wound immediately behind the eye of the hook. A long-flued hackle is wound in immediately behind the blob of fur, shiny side upwards, the tip curving over the eye. Wind in three turns and tie in behind the hackle. Clip off excess fibres.

Funnel the hackles forward over the hook eye with thumb and forefinger. With the hackle at 45 degrees over the eye of the hook, bind over the roots to secure.

Tie in whisks for the tail, tied a little way round the bend of the hook. Then a thin body of the dub of your choice may be added. Whip finish with the silk and tail slightly round the bend of the hook.

Then clip a small V out of the top of the hackle for the dun and straight across for the spinner because the fly is to be fished upside down. Patterson explains how:

> If you find it easy to tie your first Funneldun, turning it upside down is the simple part. You need only do two things in the vice. When you tie in the tail tie it in a little way round the bend. But not too much, otherwise the fly will rest on the body, rather than on the tail tips. While the fly is still in the vice, cut out a small V by clipping off a few of the hackle flues at the base from the top side of the hackle. This will be

the underside of the fly when you chuck it on the table and it flips (monotonously) upside down.

GOLD-RIBBED HARE'S EAR

The Hare's Ear, with modifications of various kinds, dates back a couple of hundred years to the Hare's Lug - 'lug' is ear - and for a fly to survive that length of time it must be good. So it is. At one time it was Halford's favourite fly. It might be worth recalling what he said:

> ...this pattern...is the most successful of modern times. From early spring to late autumn it is one of the most killing of all the duns and is, besides, to be recommended for bulging or tailing fish. It is probably taken for the sub-imago emerging from the larval envelope of the nymph just risen to the surface.[6]

There are two dressings of the Gold-Ribbed Hare's Ear which are subject to a good deal of argument. Courtney Williams explains:

> To sum up, the Gold Ribbed Hare's Ear tied as a winged floater and fished on the surface is a passable copy of an olive dun, especially when tied in the Ogden manner with a sparsely dubbed body which gives the fly a slender appearance. Dressed, as was the original pattern, with a dubbed body and a thorax and hackle of fur, it is probably the best suggestion extant of an olive nymph in the act of hatching, and fished in this form either in the surface or a little below it, it is a fly which for this purpose has no equal.

These are the two dressings:

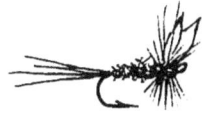

THE WINGED GRHE

Hook: 14-16.
Tail: three or four honey dun fibres.
Body: dubbed hare's fur, ribbed with fine gold wire or with fine gold tinsel.
Wing: pale starling.
Hackle: honey dun or grizzle.

THE UNWINGED GRHE

Hook: 14-16.
Tail: three or four fibres from the dark fur at the base of the hare's ear.
Body: the same as the winged fly, hare's fur ribbed with gold wire or fine gold tinsel.
Head: pick out long guard hairs from the dubbing with a needle to suggest the nymphs legs or the struggle that is taking place asthe sub-imago tries to work its way out.

Halford used the Winged GRHE, which he described as 'the most killing of all the duns'. Why, then, did he give up using it? The reason for this is found in another of his books.[7]

The Dry Fly

He was fishing the Test. He had on a Gold-Ribbed Hare's Ear, the winged version. He saw a movement by the far bank and put his fly over it and it was taken by a trout. Then more flies began to hatch. They were iron blues. Still keeping on his GRHE, he cast to the rise, took six trout, returned several more, and then stopped fishing.

> ...and during the whole time no fly except iron blues were seen and yet everyone of the fish hooked or killed took the gold ribbed hare's ear which by no possible stretch of the imagination can be considered an imitation of the blueish-tinged wings and purple body of the iron blue.

That could only mean one thing. The trout took the Hare's Ear under the impression they were taking the hatching nymph, the nymph at the point of ecdysis, and even if the dun was half out of the nymphal skin the trout was certainly taking it as an emerging nymph. According to Halford's rigid dry fly code, the Gold-Ribbed Hare's Ear was therefore not a dry fly; or as Vincent Marinaro said wryly many years later, 'it wasn't dry enough'.

It's a sad story. It was, after all, a fly that at one time Halford was very fond of. He once said that if he had to choose one fly of all the others he would choose the Gold-Ribbed Hare's Ear. Now he could no longer continue to use it. He deleted it from his list. It was the kind of thing that inevitably was bound to happen sooner or later if you make rigid rules about dry fly fishing.

It is difficult to decide whether to use the GRHE without wings, which makes it more of a nymph pattern, or a winged fly that might suggest the nymph in a further stage towards the sub-imago, which can be politely called an emerger.

THE IMPRESSIONISTS

THE GREENWELL

Colonel Harding had a considerable affection for the Greenwell which 'as a general pattern, could represent a number of olive duns and the darker pale wateries.' He gave special instructions about the dressing and the spread of the whisks symmetrically from the top of the hook shank, which I take it meant what we now call 'tied outrigger style'. He warned against getting the whisks damaged in the small compartments of dry fly boxes.

Here is his original dressing:

Hook: 14-16.
Tying silk: yellow or primrose (which goes greenish when wet). The tying silk is used to make the body of the fly.
Whisks: bright olive cock.
Body: tying silk, waxed with cobbler's wax or harness maker's wax, according to the depth of colour required to give it an olive tint. As the season advances the silk is less waxed so that its colour shall not be so dark.
Ribbing: fairly close turns of fine gold wire.
Legs or Hackle: dark 'furnace' cock hackle. The furnace hackle is very dark blue or black in the centre with reddish to honey colour at the points.
Wings: hen blackbird (primaries) for the early season fly. Starling, dark to light, as the season goes on. The wings are the conventional 'Halford type'.

The Dry Fly

However Harding was open minded on the subject:

> ...there is a large and successful school of fly fishers who question the necessity for winging a fly at all. A hackle of a colour and density which represents the combined effect of the legs and the wings of the natural fly is considered to represent the fly more accurately on the water and makes the fly lighter in weight and easier to fish. Practical experience goes far to support the view of this school.

All the same he thought that long-winged flies such as the blue-winged olive, the 'large blue-winged' pale watery and the larger olives could be better represented by wings, in shape and especially in colour, of the conventional type. A winged fly could be perfectly well dressed using single folds of feather, 'and this method is more durable.'

The story of the Greenwell starts in May, 1854, when Canon Greenwell of Durham was fishing the Tweed for trout without much success. He did not have an artificial which matched the fly on the water, probably a large dark olive. He captured one of the natural flies, took it to a professional flydresser, James Wright of Sprouston, near Kelso, and asked if he could match it. Wright produced a fly, Greenwell used it, caught large numbers of trout, and they had a celebration dinner. Greenwell asked Wright the name of the fly and Wright, according to the story, replied that obviously it must be Greenwell's Glory. Loud cheers and applause.

Wright's inspiration on the spur of the moment was superb but being a professional flydresser he would certainly have known that Bainbridge (1816) and Blacker (1843) both gave tyings of flies that were very similar to the Greenwell, using yellow silk bodies and starling wings.

These were the popular flies of the time and it is most unlikely that Wright would have invented a completely new fly when he had some perfectly good patterns at his finger tips. Nothing, however, even the facts, should be allowed to spoil a good after-dinner story and the immortality it has given to the Greenwell's Glory.

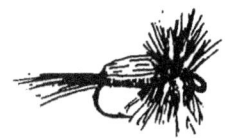

THE HUMPY

A remarkable American fly which for some curious reason has at times a considerable attraction for the trout. Fished dry on a Devon lake it rose three fish in an hour and during the mayfly on the Test it took a big rainbow when conventional mayflies had been ignored.

It looks like a bug or a beetle, possibly a small cockchafer or a bloated sedge. The Americans say it is good also when there are grasshoppers about but because in England we've killed off most of our grasshoppers with farm chemicals, that doesn't work. A wise and wizened water keeper, a friend of mine, held a Humpy in his hand for some time, turning it over and over and looking at it from all angles. Eventually he ventured the opinion that it might possibly be taken as a liver pellet.

Being made almost entirely of elk hair it floats beautifully and is excellent for drift fishing, either cruising down rivers or fishing the drift on the big natural lakes of Scotland and Ireland. It has a fairly close relation, also an American fly, called the Goofus Bug, and another with the more prosaic title of a Horner Deer Hair. However, this is the Humpy, as far as I have been able to be certain of the dressing:

The Dry Fly

Hook: almost any size from about 16 to 10, according to taste.
Tail: tie in a tail, also according to your taste, of elk hair fibres.
Body: wind on a nice chunky body of primrose silk, or similar. When the fly is complete this will be the underbody to the elk hair, only seen from below.
Wings: take a nice long piece of elk hair, tie in the tips as wings in a V-shape, bring the rest of the elk hair back and tie it down by the tail, then pull back the rest of the elk hair and tie it off just behind the wings and trim.
Hackle: grizzle and brown cock hackle tied in together, thickly, both in front and behind the wings.

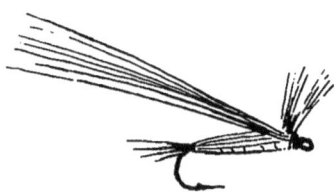

This is the way it should look when you have tied in the wings

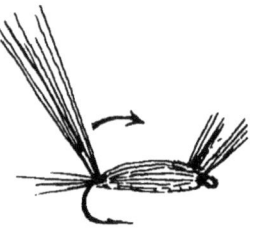

Tie off the elk hair at the tail and take it back again and tie off at the head. After this has been done, tie in the hackle thickly both in front and behind the wing.

THE IRON BLUE

A legendary fly for those who have read Harry Plunket Greene's classic adventure story of fishing in Germany, Scotland, Ireland, Blagdon, the Bourne and the Test. It is only printed here because it allows me to quote once again the most lyrical description of a dry fly ever written. Here it is, from Greene's *Where the Bright Waters Meet*:

> It is no doubt imagination but the Iron Blue always seems to me to be happier and keener and to have better manners than all the rest. He is an aristocrat, a prince on the wing, far above the world of underwater hacklers, as he sails down serene upon the stream, oblivious to rain or wind or sun, above board in his every thought and ready to work for you again and again until he disintegrates and falls to pieces from exhaustion.

But what fly? Greene never gave a dressing, never tied his own, always talked about his Iron Blue Quill, which he probably bought in dozens from tackle shops in Winchester or Stockbridge. No good asking them now. Greene died in 1936 after a wonderful and famous career as a concert singer. I suspect his Iron Blue Quill was something like this:

The Dry Fly

Greene's Iron Blue

Hook: 16.
Tying silk: crimson.
Tail: blue dun fibres.
Body: stripped peacock herl dyed a very dark blue, sometimes called an inky blue.
Wings: starling, dyed inky blue.
Hackle: inky blue dun.

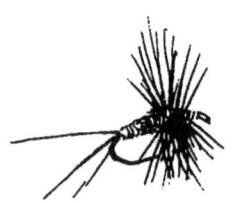

Skues' Iron Blue

Skues had a good pattern of the Iron Blue, indeed several, most if not all fished wet as part of his campaign to restore the use of the wet fly on the chalkstreams. Fished in the surface film the above is a very good emerger pattern (see dressing opposite).

If you need a spinner then probably the best is the Pheasant Tail with a blue dun hackle, a body from the dark herl of the centre of a cock pheasant's tail ribbed fine gold wire and with three long tail fibres tied spread.

Skues' Iron Blue dressing:

Hook: 14 or 16.
Body: mole's fur dubbed on claret or crimson tying silk leaving a couple of turns of bare silk at the tail.
Whisks: two or three strands of white or pale blue dun cock feathers tied spread.
Head hackle: dark blue dun.

HOUGHTON RUBY

Another of William Lunn's beautiful patterns. It is intended to imitate the spinner of the iron blue.

Hook: 16 or 18.
Tail: three long white hackle fibres spread wide.
Body: red silk underlay showing through a red cock hackle stalk wound over it.
Wings: two light blue hackle points at right angles to the hook shank.
Hackle: bright red cock.

An improvement might be the use of synthetic white hackle fibres spread wide as outriggers.

THE DRY FLY

DARK WATCHET

Another good North Country fly which does very well as an emerger of the iron blue. I knew it many years ago on the Wharfe and the Ure when it was always fished upstream, mostly sinking on a long drift, sometimes deliberately sunk by a jerk, sometimes floating dead drift. The best fishermen on these rivers used to play it, sometimes sinking and giving a flick to suggest the nymph, sometimes swirling it up to the surface, very skilful and fascinating to watch. I was never as good as that, mostly fishing it as a dead drift with a jerk here and there which used to sink it. Those were the days when paraffin was used as a floatant but most of us didn't use it partly because it wouldn't stop the fly sinking but partly because of the oil smears coming off on the water. If you wanted to use a floater then a couple of flicks on a false cast would do the trick. We always used hen hackled flies from a shop at Hawes, but in the south many years later I used to tie cock hackles which would give it a very good float.

Hook: 10, 12, 14.
Body: mole-coloured fur dubbed thinly on orange tying silk.
Head hackle: dark blue dun, almost black.

One of the many variants used mole-coloured fur dubbed on scarlet tying silk with two turns of silk exposed at the tail. I suspect the number of different dressings of this fly is because it dates back many hundreds of years. The name comes from the word 'watchet' which in medieval times was the colour of light blue cloth; hence a dark watchet, meaning a dark blue.

Lane's Emerger

Joscelyn Lane, writing at some time in the 1950s, produced a number of interesting patterns for lake fishing, generally for use on the big natural lochs of Scotland and Ireland, either for dry flies or emerger patterns. His observation of a hatching nymph is worth quoting:

> Not long ago I was fortunate enough to get an exceptionally close view of that exquisite little water miracle, as Skues called it, of a dun in the act of hatching. My boat was anchored in a backwater. It was an early summer's day, cloudy, with bright intervals, and I was gazing curiously over the side of my boat into the water, when up came a nymph right under my nose. I settled down to view the whole drama.
> The upper part of its body appeared above the surface, supported on its olive-yellow legs, and its tail end remained submerged. I watched carefully... The thorax began to swell and the head emerged and after that followed a confused medley of movements most difficult to analyse in detail. A crumpled wing appeared and then something went wrong and the other one stayed put. Round and round the little creature - or should I say creatures? - rotated slowly on the surface film and eventually the other wing broke loose. The body suddenly seemed to grow ridiculously long, until insect and shuck became distinguishable separately, and meanwhile the wings had risen to full length!

Lane's emerger pattern was based on that or a similar experience. He calls it a Hatching Lake Olive:

Hook: 12 or 10.
Tying silk: golden olive but later he says primrose.
Whisks: four strands of hare's ear- fur about 1/4 inch long.
Body: dubbing from the root of a hare's ear, rather thin, tapered at the tail end.
Rib: gold wire on body only.
Thorax: of the same fur picked out with a dubbing needle from the lower part of the thorax so that the fibres point in all directions.

The dressing is similar in many ways to the Gold-Ribbed Hare's Ear, which he discusses. He makes the point that his Hatching Lake Olive is based on the close up of the nymph in the early stage of hatching and therefore dispenses with any idea that there should be an attempt to suggest the wings, as with the winged GRHE.

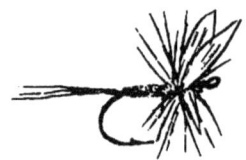

LECKFORD OLIVE DUN

Similar in many ways to Halford's Rough Olive this is much simpler and easier to tie. It is a good impressionist fly and will stand in for almost every dun in the river:

Hook: 14.
Body: medium olive fur.

Tail: three whisks the same colour as the body.
Hackle: cock hackle the same colour.
Wing: starling primary.

The fly was first tied by Kim Debenham, water keeper at the Leckford Estate water on the Test for many years and his olive dun has taken more big fish than most other patterns.

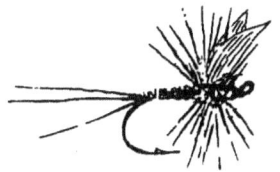

LUNN'S OLIVE DUN

Mick Lunn, the experienced Test riverkeeper from Stockbridge has the ability of being able to take ideas from many sources and convert them together into something new and interesting. His olive dun has been influenced by several olives, including the forward slanting wings of the Mole Fly, but it is an original impressionist pattern in its own right. Of all olive patterns this is one of the simplest to dress.

Hook: 14 or 16.
Tail: fibres from an olive cock.
Body: peacock quill dyed medium olive.
Hackle: olive cock; rather sparse.
Wings: medium starling tied sloping well forward.

This pattern can be used to suggest most of the olives and in slightly paler colours it also imitates the pale wateries.

An alternative dressing for the Test is the Brown Upright which has echoes of a Devon pattern, a hackled fly:

Hook: 14 or 16.
Body: stripped peacock quill and a small round blob of hare's fur just behind the hackle.
Tail: buff cock fibres.
Hackle: a mix of red and buff cock.

LUNN'S PARTICULAR

Created by William Lunn as an olive spinner, it has a wider scope. Waller Hills says it's good for taking duns as well as spinners - it was named 'Particular' as it was to be used when trout were being particular about what they were taking - and Hills went on to say that if he had to be limited to one fly then he would choose this. It is a little out of fashion these days, for fashions in flies come and go like most fashions, but Waller Hills' opinion is as good now as it was fifty years ago.

Hook: 14
Body: undyed hackle stalk from red cock (Rhode Island Red)
Tail: four long fibres of red cock
Wings: two medium hackle points tied on flat to suggest the spent fly
Hackle: red cock with a clipped V underneath.

The Impressionists

William Lunn and his descendants will always be linked to the history of the Houghton Club. The club was founded in 1822, it has nearly 15 miles of some of the best water of the river Test. It was the centre of the Halford-Marryat researches at BossingtonMill, 1880-1886, which established what was then the revolutionary dry fly code, and three generations of the Lunn family, known worldwide, have been riverkeepers on the Houghton water from 1887 to 1994.

William Lunn began work at Houghton in 1887 and retired 55 years later. He was a practical naturalist and a splendid flytyer. Waller Hills wrote about his life and times in *River Keeper*, published in 1934. His son Alfred took over in 1932 and one of his many achievements was to substitute borehole water for stream water in the rearing of fry which increased the survival rate from 50 to 80 per cent. Alfred's son, Mick, took over in 1963, retiring in 1994, having made considerable advances in modern methods of fish farming and producing yet more admirable dry fly patterns.

The Big Mayfly

The first new designer flies for the big mayfly came from an American, Lee Wulff. He was a professional guide, lecturer, and a great conservationist in the days before conservation became important. Wulff was anxious to create what he called 'a buggier-looking, heavier-bodied fly' that would mean a better mouthful for trout, especially trout feeding on the big American mayfly, the Green Drake. It turned out to be a very important fly for Britain's even bigger and buggier big mayfly, *Ephemera danica*.

GREY WULFF

Many Americans disliked this 'bigger and buggier' fly of the 1930s on sight. Preston Jennings, doyen of the close imitation school, said that the Grey Wulff did not imitate any known insect and he couldn't imagine it was any good. Even stronger criticism came from some of the traditionalists on the Test when it was first seen in England. 'Wouldn't be seen dead with it' was a typical comment. The fly did not appeal to the purist. It appealed to the trout. By the late 40s and 50s it was in most of our tackle shops. What was the attraction?

The original Grey Wulff is now in the American Museum of Fly Fishing. One very noticeable feature is the long thick tail or whisks, far longer than the *setae* of the natural fly. The effect of this is to lift the body and the hook of the fly above the level of the water. The hackle at the head of the fly gives a good imprint. The flare of the spreading fibre wings, slanted forward, give a good image, the so-called ghost wing, as the fly enters the trout's window. However you look at it, the imprint, the ghost wings, the way the hook is lifted out of the water, all these are as near perfect as possible in creating an image that the trout will recognise as a natural fly.

This is the dressing:

Hook: 10 or even 8, long shank or standard.
Tail: long, thick, natural brown hackles. Or long, thin hackle point. Must be stiff to help lift the hook clear of the water.
Body: grey Angora yarn.
Wings: natural bucktail, white-tipped, sloping well forward beyond the eye of the hook, the fibres flared out.
Head hackle: blue-grey cock.

It is important that the wing should not be split but flared, fanlike. There are various alternative dressings, but I doubt whether small changes are important. In smaller sizes it does well for all the olives.

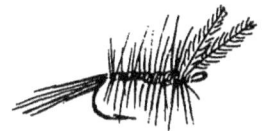

SHADOW MAYFLY

Meanwhile, dedicated followers of Harding on the Hungerford water of the Kennet were experimenting with a hackled fly. Hackles create an interesting illusion of something alive, maybe from the light that comes through, maybe from the impression of movement, maybe from a fuzzy imprint and light pattern seen in the trout's mirror. For whatever reason a hackled fly has been a basic artificial for several hundred years. Thomas Barker, adviser on flies to Izaak Walton, wrote in 1651:

> Now to shew how to make Flies; learn to make two Flies, and make all; that is, the Palmer ribbed with silver or gold, and the May Flie; these are the ground of all Flies.

The rods on the Kennet in the 40s and 50s must have had something like that very much in mind; the Palmer and the Mayfly, 'the ground of all flies'. They tried a Palmer fly, hackled from head to bend, and a little way behind the head they tied in two stubs of hackle with the tops cut off to give the impression of a ghost wing. They tried it out and it worked.

No eyewitness account survives, as far as I know. Those involved in the discussions about the vision of the trout and the theories of Harding were Borlase Eady, Dr Cecil Terry, and J. Arthur Palethorpe of Hungerford Priory. It was Palethorpe who introduced the fly to the professional flydresser, Peter Deane, who was surprised at the sight of it. Later he wrote:

> In the hand it looks nothing like the real mayfly and it took me some 16 years after I first tied it before I had sufficient confidence to use it, and what a surprise when I did! It is most effective and creates the illusion or impression of a fly.

Here is the original dressing:

> **Hook:** 10 or 8 standard length or a longshank 10.
> **Body and Tail:** none.
> **Wings:** two large brown cock hackles tied in fairly well from the eye of the hook, leaning slightly forward. Trim the points square so you get stubby wings.
> **Hackle:** grizzle cock palmered thinly from the eye to the bend of the hook.

It is important that the hackling should not be tied in too close with the fibres jammed up tightly together, as you often see them in the shops. Light must come through. A thick bunch of hackles all stuck close together will not make a very good imprint.

In his book, Peter Deane suggests that the points of the hackle should be trimmed very lightly, using only the points of the scissors. This makes it a bouncer kind of fly that will move more easily in a wind.

The Impressionists

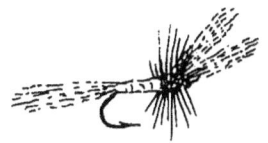

Goddard's Mayfly:
The Poly May Dun

This is a beautiful fly to look at, golden wings and golden tail, a real golden mayfly, one of John Goddard's best and simplest creations.

It is, incidentally, fascinating to have followed Goddard's development as a flydresser over many years. It is in a way a kind of pilgrim's progress from tying close imitations of the natural insect to a movement towards impressionism, if that is the right word. Certainly towards designs that create the illusion of a fly rather than a copy. Of his Poly May Dun he writes:

> It is dressed to represent the emerging mayfly on the surface. This was achieved by tying a bunch of calf's tail used to form the wings as a tag about half the shank length of the hook beyond the bend, this then represented the partly emerging shuck of the mayfly. This calf's tail is then bound along the top of the shank almost to the eye where it is turned up and divided into the required V shaped wings with a figure of eight tying, the wings pointing slightly forward over the eye.

Over two seasons he experimented with different coloured wings and finally decided on pale gold.

> ...as I had noticed on bright days the naturals when hatching seemed to transmit a golden glow despite the fact that the wings of the naturals, when examined, appeared

greenishblue with dark patches. While the final pattern close up seemed to bear little or no resemblance to the natural - on the water it was extremely difficult to tell them apart.

This is the dressing:

Hook: wide gape 10 or 12.
Tying silk: strong white.
Shuck and Wings: a bunch of white calf's tail dyed pale gold. The ends are tied on the top of the hook shank projecting over the eye to form V-shaped wings sloping forward.
Body: cream coloured polypropylene yarn (poly yarn), no ribbing.
Hackles: two turns of black cock on either side of the wing root.

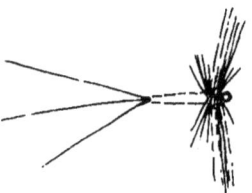

Goddard's Mayfly Spinner:
POLY MAY SPINNER

This is basically the same design as the dun except it has long tails, a white body and a mixture of black and white calf's tails for the wings. These Wulff-style shaped wings are tied in with a much wider V so that when it lands on the water surface it tends to cock one side or the other so that one wing stays flat on the surface while the other is cocked vertically. This is what happens so often during a fall of the natural spinners.

Hook: Roman Moser arrow point hooks size 10 or 12.
Tying silk: black.
Tails: three long nylon brush filaments coloured black with a waterproof felt pen.
Wing: black and white calf's tail fibres well mixed and tied in a wide V; Body: white polypropylene yarn.
Hackle: black cock hackles short in flew, two turns behind wing and two in front.

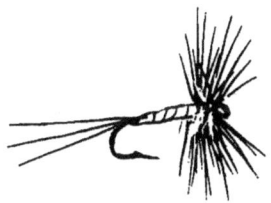

MICK LUNN'S SHAVING BRUSH

Created by the third generation of the Lunns of the Houghton Club on the Test, Mick Lunn's comically named mayfly does look a little like a shaving brush with the grey-black wings tied well forward. A small alteration and it changes from a dun to a spinner.

Hook: 12 or 10 longshank.
Whisks: two or three fibres.
Body: thin white wool ribbed with black or brown tying silk.
Wings: grey and black hackle mixed fairly thickly and tied well forward for the dun; grey hackle tied forward and divided for the spinner.

A useful development might be to have synthetic whisks tied outrigger style.

ALSTON'S HACKLE

Another Test favourite during the big mayfly, slightly reminiscent of the French Partridge but with three soft hackles instead of two.

Hook: 10 or 8.
Body: yellow raffia.
Tail: three strands from the centre of a cock pheasant tail.
Back head hackle: English partridge dyed yellow.
Centre head hackle: French partridge dyed yellow.
Front hackle: light breast feather from the English partridge.

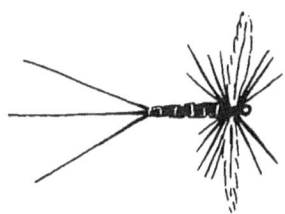

Black Drake

This is a Leckford mayfly which suggests the spinner but is also good when duns are on the water. It is one of the few flies these days which has a rubber body.

Hook: 10 or 12.
Body: made from tight turns of rubber sheeting.
Tail: three strands from the centre tail of a cock pheasant.
Hackle: dark badger cock.
Wings: hackle points or shaped white cock tied spent.

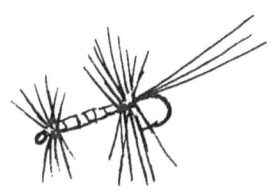

Fore and Aft Mayfly

A fly tilted down at the head and up at the tail to copy the position on the water of the natural mayfly. David Jacques tied it after lying flat on a wooden bridge over the Test at Marsh Court watching the real mayflies and the artificial French Partridge which he threw in so they floated down the river together. The French Partridge tail

The Dry Fly

sagged. The tail of the natural mayflies were higher than the head. So he copied them.

> **Hook:** size not given, probably 10 or 8 longshank.
> **Whisks:** three or four fibres from cock pheasant's tail.
> **Body:** natural raffia over red-brown floss silk. The floss silk is used to build up the body shape. Three or four rings of the floss are exposed at the end of the hook.
> **Hackle at the bend of the hook:** a large stiff olive cock feather.
> **Hackle at the head:** a much smaller feather, a light greenish-yellow olive cock.

After trying out the Fore and Aft he wrote:

> 'with a sense of losing an old and valued friend I divorced the French partridge from my mayflies for ever.'[8]

MICROFLIES

The microflies of the Upper Itchen at Martyr Worthy are unique. So is the man who ties them. Ron Holloway has been a dry fly fisherman for 40 years and the last 25 years of them as riverkeeper at Martyr Worthy and over that time his fly patterns have become smaller and smaller. You may find an occasional 18 among them but most are at least size 20, some even smaller. Holloway explains why:

> The Upper Itchen is a pure chalkstream, pristine, clear and shallow. On the Test or Kennet the waters are coloured for

most of the season and so a 14 or 16 will readily take the naive stocked rainbows or browns. Upper Itchen trout are wild and small. The average catch size at Martyr Worthy is 1lb 3oz compared with fish-farm stocked fish of other waters.

One of the interesting things about these very small flies is that Holloway seems indifferent about the colour.

> Few if any of my flies are similar to any of the standard dry flies which are available in tackle shops. Yet for my fishing on the Upper Itchen I find these little flies work very well. My own dry fly philosophy is that accurate and delicate presentation, the size of fly and the shape are the most important factors to be taken into consideration. I wouldn't claim that any one of these flies are tied to any original pattern, or personal design, because there is nothing very unique in any of them, they are solely flies tied which can sometimes fool the fish on my river...

And he goes on to emphasise the important things by underlining them: <u>shape</u>, <u>size</u> and <u>accurate and delicate presentation</u>.

Ron Holloway, fishing his microflies on the Itchen

Here are some of Holloway's flies:

LARGE DARK OLIVE / SPRING OLIVE

Hook: 20 or 22.
Whisks: short and grey colour.
Body: grey fur.
Wings: dark olive.
Hackle: dark olive.

MEDIUM OLIVE DUN

Hook: 20 or 22.
Whisks: honey dun longer than the shank.
Body: peacock quill.
Wings: light starling.
Hackle: honey dun.

BLUE-WINGED OLIVE DUN

Hook: 20 or 22.
Whisks: short blue dun.
Body: grey fur.
Wings: two short hackle points.
Hackle: Blue dun, quite short.

SPENT OLIVE / OLIVE SPINNER

Hook: 20.
Similar tyings to the duns except that the wings are hackle points and the whisks longer, while some of the bodies are orange silk and others olive silk.

The Impressionists

Emergers

Nymph shapes, dark olive bodies, short whisks, and a tiny upright wing of a few fibres, suggesting the full wing still to come.

It might be of interest to mention that Martyr Worthy was not named because someone was worthy of martyrdom. Martyr comes from one of the descendants of the Normans who owned the fishing, a knight called Le Martre, and Worthy is most likely Old English 'woröig' probably meaning place or enclosure.[9]

The Upper Itchen was where Edward Grey (Viscount Grey of Falloden) used to escape to from the Foreign Office to go fishing. He had a fishing hut in the woods, but sadly all that remains of the hut are the stone floor and the chimney stack.

Midges

Chalkstream fishermen are, by tradition, inclined to overlook the midge, that is to say the non-biting midge belonging to the chironomid family. It is a pity that they don't fish it more frequently as midges sometimes hatch in huge numbers on the Test and Kennet, often in sizes that are so small the fisherman can't tell what is happening.

Wherever you go on stillwaters, from the Irish loughs to Blagdon and to the smallest of small ponds, there will be a midge rise, sometimes at mid-day, sometimes in the evening. The first fisherman I know of who exploited the midge was Dr H.A. Bell (1888-1974) of Blagdon who first fished a simple wet fly pattern known as the Buzzer in the 1920s. Since then patterns have multiplied. One of the best I know for fishing an emerger midge is John Goddard's, which is fished as a dry fly.

MIDGE EMERGER

A good deal of work has been done, especially in America, to suggest the hatching mayflies and olives, but there is only one pattern I know which imitates the hatching midge. This is John Goddard's Suspender Midge Pupa.

There is a charming story which relates how the design of this fly came about by accident. John Goddard, Brian Clarke and Neil Patterson all fish the same beat of the Kennet and all were interested in tying a hatching nymph pattern which involved tying a ball of closed cell ethafoam on the back of the nymph to keep it afloat.

Goddard was tying one of these floating nymphs when by accident he tied in one of the little white balls too close to the eye of the hook. He removed it from the vice and tossed it away on the desk. Then something important happened:

> While dressing another pattern I idly glanced at the discarded one from some distance and it suddenly struck me that the white ball sitting almost over the eye of the hook closely resembled the bunch of white breathing filaments on the top of a natural midge pupa.

This was what he had been trying to create for years and there it was, suddenly, right in front of him. He and Neil Patterson tied some of these and found them, Goddard says 'enormously successful'.

THE IMPRESSIONISTS

His emerging midge was originally developed for fishing on the big lakes and reservoirs. Recently, he says, the pattern has been proved to be very killing on rivers on size 18 hooks. He now believes that:

> ...on most rivers these little natural midges are far more numerous than the *ephemeroptera* of upwinged flies. Despite this they have until quite recently been ignored by river fly fishers.

This is the standard pattern for both rivers and lakes:

Hook: generally size 18 for rivers, larger for lakes.
Body: floss of a colour to match the naturals, ribbed.
Tail: a few white filaments.
Thorax: dark brown condor herl.
Floater: a small ball of white ethafoam enclosed in white nylon mesh (nylon stockings or tights).

For lake fishing Goddard has also found that his Suspender Midge is most successful during heavy hatches of the natural if several are tied on as droppers quite close together and cast to the rise. He has found that a group of flies are inclined to attract the trout more effectively than singles when the trout are feeding right in the surface. The Suspender is of course always fished as a dry fly and the flyfisher now has the advantage of having a pattern for an emerging midge as well as the standard patterns for an emerging dun.

The Dry Fly

Black Duck Fly

The Duck Fly, similar in many ways to the Blae and Black, is a midge fly for the loughs of Ireland and Scotland. There are times when the midge on these great lakes hatch in millions. Once on Lough Sheelin, many years ago, before it was polluted by the pig farms, a hatch of midge was so prolific that the insects seemed to hang like a moving grey curtain between me and the sun. What a day that was for the Duck Fly.

> **Hook:** 16 to 12.
> **Body:** black or very dark green, almost black, thickened towards the shoulder.
> **Wings:** two dun or cream hackle points tied sloping back from the thickened shoulder and at an angle so the points will rest on the water with the body visible between.
> **Hackle:** rusty dark cock, black cock or dark blue dun tied in front of the wings.

Various lakes have their own pet ways of fishing the Black Duck Fly. My uncle, Willie Cox, always fished it wet and moving, my father fished it dry and floating from a boat with only an occasional twitch. If you fish it wet, clip the hackle both on top and the bottom so all that is left is a few sparse legs. Another way is to fish it dry as a top dropper or in the surface film for the middle and point. A most versatile fly.

The Impressionists

Blagdon Green Midge

The Blagdon Green Midge dates from sometime in the 1920s or 30s, originally fished wet by my uncle Willie Cox and dry by my father who anointed it with paraffin. It has a particular charm for me because I caught my first Blagdon trout on a Green Midge when I fished there as a school boy with my father in the late 1920s. There is nothing very special about the dressing but clearly it is a good imprint for a midge.

> **Hook:** 14 or 16.
> **Body:** emerald green wool ribbed with very fine gold wire.
> **Hackle:** white cock or hen, sloping slightly back towards the body.

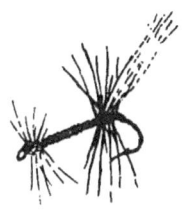

The Janus

The Janus is an exceptional black gnat created by, among others, Hal Thirlway, Ken Fox, and Brenda Elphick. The fly floats tail high in the same manner as David Jacques' mayfly. The hackle tied at the bend of the hook is always longer in the fibre than the one at the eye.

Hook: 22.
Body: slim black silk.
Rear hackle: red cock, normal size.
Wings: five long Plymouth Rock or cree fibres fanned out and tied in close to the rear hackle.
Shoulder hackle: short badger cock.

Test it in a bowl of water to make sure that the fly cocks upright. Hal Thirlaway wrote about the Janus in the *Flyfishers' Journal*:

> In 1969 Ken Fox agreed with me to fish Piscatorial Society waters using only this fly (the Janus) and to 'renew hope' not by changing pattern but by changing size. One summer evening Ken was landing fish at Axford (River Kennet) during a classic BWO hatch. Below him Shrimp Hordern was frustrated. At last he called 'what fly Ken?' Ken couldn't face 'a knotted black gnat with tails'. Joining me in the Red Lion afterwards he urged us to seek a more acceptable name for our fly. The answer was obvious that evening - Janus.[10]

BLACK HACKLE

A very useful black palmer fly which is really tied to suggest a bunch of mating midges but is equally good for reed smuts, houseflies, black gnats, and almost any dark coloured insect. Always fished dry, a simple Black Hackle should always be somewhere in your box.

Hooks: 14 to 18 or 20.
Body: black cock hackle wound from head to tail.

OLIVE QUILL

Edward Grey, (1862–1933) wrote a book on flyfishing which was first published in 1899 and has had several editions and reprints over the years. He was one of Britain's great Foreign Secretaries, holding office from 1905 to 1916, and he later became Viscount Grey of Fallodon He is probably best remembered for his comment on the outbreak of the First World War. At night, on the day war was declared, looking out of the windows of the Cabinet room in Downing Street towards the lights of Pall Mall, he said 'The lamps are going out all over Europe; we shall not see them lit again in our lifetime.'

Fisherman will remember him for his charm, wit and perception - and for his Olive Quill. They will also remember his famous description of fishing in the Highlands:

> The pure act of breathing at such times seems glorious. People talk about being a child of nature and moments such as these there are times when it is possible to feel so; to know the full joy of animal life - to desire nothing beyond. There are times when I have stood still for joy of it all, on my way through the wild freedom of a Highland moor, and felt the wind and looked upon the mountains and water and light and sky, till I felt conscious only of the strength of a mighty current of life, which swept away all consciousness of self, and made me a part of all I beheld.

As well as fishing for salmon on the Rosehall water of the Cassley, he also fished the Lochy, Spean and Tweed. He had a small cottage on the banks of the Upper Itchen to which he could escape from the Foreign Office at weekends and knot on his favourite Orange Quill. The dressing is very simple. He bought his flies from Hammond of Winchester, not having much time to tie his own.

Hook: 16, sometimes 14.
Tail: three fibres of olive cock.
Body: stripped peacock quill dyed olive.
Wing: starling primary.

Grey fished the Itchen at a time when there was a rigid dry fly code, enforced by Halford's disciples, but he took little notice of such restrictions. The flies he carried included the Iron Blue, a Red Quill as well as the Orange Quill, a Sedge, and a Big Mayfly, but he would also fish a Black Hackle tied with a hen feather which he fished wet where he felt it was appropriate, following the example of Skues.

Orange Partridge

When I was a boy, fishing the Yorkshire becks, I almost always had an Orange Partridge as the dropper fly on my two-fly cast. It was my father's favourite fly for upstream wet fly fishing on our beck, a small rocky stream flowing fast down from the wolds, rippling along between spiky barriers of rock, smoothing out and eddying into quiet pools where there would be so often a trout behind a stone. You fished quickly, walking upstream, flicking the fly into the likely places, never letting it rest too long on the water, lifting off and covering another foot or so, lifting off again, moving up, covering fresh water.

All the time I noticed that the Orange Partridge, the bob fly, would always lie flat on the surface of the water, and it would stay afloat, flat, hugging the water surface until it was pulled under by a curl and suck of the current. Then, as I lifted off again, flicked it behind, flicked it forward, covering fresh water, it would fall as light as a feather and float down on the surface, a draggled insect of some kind, until the water and the point fly, the pull of one and the weight of the other, would capsize it and take it below the surface out of sight.

But the rises would always seem to come as the the fly fell and rode the surface of the water. Time and time again that was when you had to be ready for the take, and in nine cases out of ten the take to the Orange Partridge came while it floated, tranquil and happy on the drift. The moment the bob fly touches the water, my father used to say, is when the trout will have a snap at it.

Many, many years later, fishing the Lambourn, just above where it comes into the Kennet, the Orange Partridge took its first chalkstream fish not with a snap but with the gentle confident suck of a trout that recognises the floating dead spinner with tousled wings and the orange body.

I never changed the dressing. You can of course make changes to your hearts content, putting on whisks for example, but I found, as Waller Hills had found, that it does not matter much. It does not seem to make much difference. If you want a good spinner pattern you can do a lot worse than transpose the wet fly Orange Partridge into the dry.

Hook: 14 or 16.
Body: orange silk.

The Dry Fly

Head hackle: small mottled feather from the back or neck of a partridge, or one of the feathers from under the wing.

Parachute Flies

One of the most remarkable of the new designs is the parachute style of dressing, developed in the 1930s when an American visitor to Scotland, William A. Brush from Detroit, called in at Alex Martin's tackle shop in Exchange Square, Glasgow and asked if they had anyone who could tie what he called a 'side hackle fly'. The request was passed to the lady flydressers in the back room and one of them, Helen Todd, tied the first parachute fly. Her method was to tie some gold twist on the hook shank, tie the hackle round it, then fasten the gold twist under the hook and lacquer it to keep it firmly in place.

A further development was to have a small metal projection, part of the hook shank, round which the hackle could be wound. These hooks were supplied by Alfred Willis of Limerick Works, Redditch. Martins sold parachute flies with a small label on the hook saying that they were patented.

There were something like 24 designs with different colours and hackles all named after conventional patterns, Grouse and Green Parachute, Olive Quill Parachute, and many others. Orders poured in from all over the world, from India, Africa, the United States and Canada. But to begin with there were many doubts, the metal spikes made the hooks too heavy, and it was not until the 50s and 60s that new ways came of dressing the fly on ordinary hooks

THE IMPRESSIONISTS

Various dressings of the parachute fly, all of them named after traditional flies, are in the shops. This is good for sales but not necessary. One type of a parachute fly will do for all. The best dressing I know is:

PARACHUTE ADAMS

Named after the dressing of the traditional Adams on page 24 it has enthusiastic followers on both sides of the Atlantic.

Hook: generally 14 but it can range from 12 to 20.
Shuck or tail: a short grizzle and brown stub to suggest the discarded shuck of the nymph.
Body: muskrat or similar dubbing.
Wing spike: an upright bunch of white calf tail tied well back from the eye of the hook.
Hackle: strip off the fluff from a good grizzle cock feather and tie it down on the body of the fly both behind and in front of the wing spike. Then wind the feather round the base of the wing spike three or four times until you get a good circular spread of hackle.

A design improvement comes from Mr E.J.T. Matthews of Winchester. Using small flies in a fading light, a wing spike of white Antron instead of calf tail improves visibility.

In conditions of bright sunlight in open country Mr Herb G. Wellington of Montana says the fly is more visible under dazzling conditions with a black wing spike.

The Dry Fly

The dressing of a Danish parachute fly is given on page 31 as it was designed as a Blue-winged Olive pattern.

In tying the Parachute Adams it is best to tie in the wing first, making quite sure that it is upright and fairly near the centre of the shank of the hook. Then tie in the tail. A good idea is to put a little celluloid varnish (vinyl cement in America) on the base of the wing and the tail. Then dub the abdomen and thorax. Tie in the grizzle cock hackle, making sure it is firmly anchored both in front and behind the wing spike before beginning the turns round the base of the wing.

The Parachute Adams will represent all the mayflies, olives, iron blues, blue-winged olives, pale wateries, duns and emergers. It has been known to take trout which have been feeding on spinners and there have been times when it has been savaged by a trout during a hatch of sedge.

The Peacock

This little nymph was originally tied as wet fly by Dave Schultz, an American fisherman, when visiting West Yellowstone. It was fished dead drift in the surface film to trout, big cutthroats, that were feeding on the nymphs but ignoring the duns. They were rolling, tailing and porpoising in pursuit of the nymphs and, says Craig Mathews, the Peacock fished dead drift to individual fish was never refused. That certainly is a claim.

For our chalkstreams I would suggest the Peacock is given a dose of floatant and fished on the surface as an emerger, a nymph about to burst out of the shuck. Hare's Ear and peacock herl do seem to have a special attraction for the trout.

Hook: 20 to 22, but at times larger (such as a 14 or 16).
Body: green peacock herl wrapped with olive tying thread from tail to head, then trimmed and tapered to a nymphal shape. A small hackle at the head would indicate an emerger.

Pheasant Tail

One of the great traditional flies, like the Greenwell, the Pheasant Tail arouses a deep emotional attachment in many experienced flyfishermen. Some use nothing else. One fisherman on the Itchen I knew, when it was leased by the Piscatorials, was a one-fly man like Threlfall. Though the Pheasant Tail was originally a spinner he used it for everything, all the duns, olives, pale wateries, iron blues, the lot. It also works wonders on nearly every river and lake in the British Isles.

The following modern dressing comes from Devon:

Hook: 14 or 16.
Tail: three herls from the centre tail of a cock pheasant.
Body: dark reddish herl from the same tail of the cock pheasant ribbed with fine gold wire.
Wing: a brassy honey dun cock.

The original, tied about 1900, used honey dun cock spade feather for the whisks. This was changed later to the pheasant tail fibres. An improvement would be to have several more long fibres

The Dry Fly

tied close together on the bend to lift the hook from the surface of the water, as with the Adams and the Grey Wulff. This would not apply to the spinner.

Poult Bloa

Another very good Yorkshire pattern, generally fished wet in the north, fished as an emerger dry fly in the south. For the change over you might like to refer back to the Orange Partridge on page 72. The name poult means a young chicken or game bird. Bloa is a dialect word, probably inherited from the Norse, meaning blue. The words are a clue to the dressing, not what the fly is supposed to represent. In fact it is a pretty good imitation of a pale watery spinner. Keep it in reserve if your standard spinners are refused.

There are several dressings. This one comes from Edmonds and Lee.

> **Head hackle:** a pale blue feather from the under coverts of a young grouse wing or alternatively a pale blue dun.
> **Body:** primrose yellow silk. I would suggest tapering the body from the head to the bend of the hook.

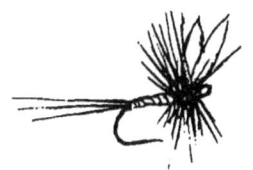

THE RED QUILL

Described by Halford as the dry fly fisherman's 'sheet anchor' wherever he fished, the Red Quill has now given way to the claims of other designs. Nevertheless, as Courtney Williams says, it is a pattern of great general ability, fished wet or dry.

Hook: 14, 16, 18.
Whisks: three fibres of red cock.
Body: stripped peacock quill from the eye of the tail feather, dyed red.
Wings: pale or medium starling.
Hackle: bright red cock.

The great American fisherman, Vincent Marinaro, said that he found the Red Quill took trout feeding on very small insects dressed on hook sizes as small as 24. See Microflies on page 62.

THE DRY FLY

THE SEDGE AND CADDIS FLIES

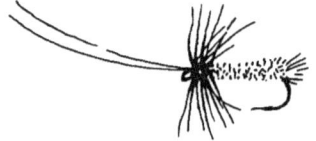

THE G&H SEDGE

(OR GODDARD'S CADDIS)

One of the most interesting and ingenious of the modern dressings, Goddard's Sedge, is simply the shape of a natural fly, body and wings combined in one, which has a very good imprint and light pattern.

Originally tied by John Goddard with his friend Cliff Henry (hence the G&H Sedge) for fishing on lakes and reservoirs where it was virtually unsinkable even in the roughest water, it was also found to be a good river fly. The Americans took it up and have named it Goddard's Caddis.

Goddard says: 'providing you have mastered the technique of spinning deerhair on a bare shank this is a relatively simple pattern to dress.' It is as follows:

Hook: longshank 8 to 12.
Tying silk: green.
Under body: dark green seal's fur, or substitute.
Body: spinnings of deer hair trimmed to shape.
Hackle: two rusty dun cock.

Not having mastered the technique of spinning deer hair I asked a professional, Craig Mathews, if I could use a quotation from his book[11] to explain how it should be done.

Good spinning deer hair that is also quite fine is the essential ingredient [and] spinning the body should be accomplished with two clumps of hair, no more or less, regardless of the size of the fly. The first clump is attached and spun where a conventional tail would be tied in, just ahead of the bend. The second clump should be packed up right against the first and should end with the front half of the hook shank showing. This may seem like too short a body but once it is trimmed it will be perfect. Not leaving adequate room for the hackle is a common error which results in a misproportioned fly. Trim the body to a caddis shape before continuing to tie in a brown hackle and two stripped brown hackle stems as antennae.

LITTLE RED SEDGE

G.E.M. Skues (1858–1949) was the most influential fisherman of his generation and his many books are still avidly read. He was the first to challenge the dry fly code on the chalkstreams, the first to urge chalkstream fishermen to return to the upstream wet fly technique when trout were feeding under the surface, and the first to tie the imitations of the ephemeropteran nymphs on which the trout were feeding. Known as 'the father of the nymph' he tied many invaluable dry fly dressings of which his Little Red Sedge was but one. It is still widely used, gives a good imprint and light pattern to the trout, and can suggest sedges of all sizes, shapes and colours. See Harding's comment on sedges on page 89.

Hook: 14 or to size.
Tying silk: hot orange rubbed with brown wax.
Body: dubbed dark hare's ear.
Body rib: fine gold wire tied in at bend.
Body hackle: deep red cock with short fibres hackled from shoulder to tail bound down by the rib.
Wing: landrail or substitute bunched and rolled, tied in sloping well back over the bend of the hook.
Front hackle: like the body hackle but with longer fibres, tied in five or six times in front of the wing.

THE BIGHORN CADDIS

I discovered this fly on the Bighorn river in the border area of Wyoming and Montana while on a fishing trip to America many years ago. There was an enormous hatch of very small dark caddis, almost black. They were riding the food stream in enormous numbers, packed in together, thick as bank holiday traffic on the Brighton road. They crawled all over me, got inside my shirt, tickled, and got squashed. I was given the fly by the guide and we had a wonderful time. I forgot to ask the name of the fly so I have called it the Bighorn Caddis. It does wonders as a very small caddis and also as a tiny black fly. This is the dressing:

Hook: 18 or 20.
Body: black thread, thickening towards the head.
Wing: a small slip of dark feather - rook or coot, lying close to the body, extending a fraction longer than the hook bend.

Head hackle: a couple of turns of black hackle, clipped close to the underpart of the hook so that the 'legs' project on either side of the hook. This keeps the fly low on the water and gives a good light pattern. If it sinks it is still lethal.

THE CAPERER

'The invaluable Caperer, greatest of summer flies' eulogised Waller Hills in his classic history of a chalkstream, *A Summer on the Test*.

One of the big sedges, the Caperer was created by William Lunn, waterkeeper for the Houghton Club on the Test for 55 years, retiring in 1932. The original pattern was winged - in those days every dry fly had to be winged - and the winged pattern is still in use but many fishermen have abandoned wings for a hackle. This is the winged fly:

Hook: 14, 12 or 10.
Body: the lower body is dark turkey tail twisted on crimson silk, the middle body is two swan feathers dyed yellow, and the top of the body, the thorax, is again dark turkey tail.
Wings: bleached coot dyed chocolate brown and tied roof, shape close to the body.
Hackle: red and black cock, mixed together, tied in front of the wings.

The Dry Fly

Guy Robinson of Leckford has a good pattern with hackle wings. Everything else is the same as the winged pattern but the hackle wings are a black cock tied in first and then a red hackle in front of it.

The hackled Caperer is in use almost everywhere, on lakes and reservoirs, on limestone, chalk and many spate rivers. It ranks, I think, alongside Skues' Little Red Sedge, as one of the two most widely-used sedge flies.

The Impressionists

Elk Hair Caddis

An attractive-looking fly, popular in the United States and one that makes a good light pattern, is the Elk Hair Caddis, designed by Al Troth. The shops sell them in different colours, which is good for trade, but what matters is not the colour but the imprint. Natural rather coarse elk hair is better than the finer hair as it flares better when the butts are tied down.

> **Hook:** from 12 to 18; Body: dubbing of brown or olive fur.
> **Body hackle:** short fibred grizzle hackle palmered from head to bend.
> **Wing:** tie a bunch of elk hair at the head, bring the thread tightly round so that the elk hair fibres flare out into the shape of the wing. The fibres should now be separate, letting the light through.

Palmer Sedge

Another new dressing, this one from Datus C. Proper, similar to all the palmer dressings such as the Bi-visible, the Threlfall, and so on, and highly effective, with a good light pattern. On the following page are Proper's instructions[12] on how it should be tied:

Body: wind a good bed of waxed silk from eye to bend. Tie in a short fibred red hackle at the bend and gold or silver wire.
Dubbing: wind in a fuzzy body of hare's ear or similar.
Hackle: wind the hackle forward to the front of the body and tie off. Then wind the ribbing wire forward in the opposite direction to secure the hackle. At the head of the fly tie in a different coloured hackle, probably grizzly.

Houghton Sedges

Typical of the care taken by Mick Lunn to make sure that his patterns suggest the many different sedges seen on the Houghton water of the Test is the fact that he has designed three different patterns - black, orange and silver - and can produce three more if they're wanted. In this he has the same thorough approach of Halford who also picked out three sedges - dark, medium and cinnamon. Here are Lunn's:

Black Sedge

Body: fibres of turkey tail dyed purple.
Wings: rook.
Hackle: black and dark red mixed.

Orange Sedge

Body: orange wool ribbed gold twist.
Wing: well blotched pheasant wing dyed yellow orange.
Hackle: two buff cock hackles.
Ribbing hackle: buff cock.

The Impressionists

Mick Lunn, third generation of riverkeepers on the Test

Silver Sedge

Body: white artificial silk.
Wing: wild duck.
Hackle: two ginger cock.
Ribbing hackle: ginger cock.

LANE'S TRIMMED HACKLE SEDGES

Joscelyn Lane specialised in dry fly and emerger fishing on lakes and lochs and produced some good sedge patterns, among others, probably rather better patterns than many of those more publicised in the following years by reservoir fishermen. He gave about seven or eight sedge patterns in his *Lake and Loch Fishing*, published by Seeley Service (undated) probably in the late 1950s.

His basic pattern, with variations for larger sedges such as medium, dark, cinnamon, and so on, was his trimmed hackle sedge which could be fished both wet and dry. His own preference, to judge from the text, would be to fish it dry.

> **Hook:** not given, suitable for the size of the natural sedge
> **Body:** tie in a long cock's hackle at a point slightly round the bend of the hook. Wind it on with coils touching one another but not overlapping and fibres vertical. Cover the whole of the body and thorax in this way, using as many hackles as necessary. Then clip off all fibres close to the quill.
> **Wing:** ship the long fibres for the space of 1½ inches from both sides of a very broad brown cock's hackle. Form them into a bunch with the butts level and tie them in at the butts at the head of the hook leaving room for the legs. Bind them down so that the hackle lies in contact with the body of the fly throughout its length. This is important. Touch tying silk with varnish. Trim off the ends of the wings beyond the bend of the hook, making the fly roughly triangular in shape, viewed both from the side and from below. [*Editor's note*: same shape as the Goddard's Caddis]
> **Leg Hackle:** three or four turns of a small cock's hackle tied with fibres radiating roughly at right angles to the shank.

Light Pattern of the Sedge

The value of the palmer hackle, the 'buzz' effect, was emphasised by Harding in discussing the important light pattern of the sedge. He wrote:

The Impressionists

The sedge fly in general can move on the surface and is not at the mercy of the current as are the ephemerid flies. In so doing it produces a long line of sparkles. As pointed out by Mr G.E.M. Skues the buzz form of dressing probably suggests this movement. By winding a hackle down the body in addition to the shoulder hackle, the length of the area of sparkles is increased and so very possibly does suggest movement. Although primarily a sedge dressing, the type is applicable to a number of other flies that appear on the water, such as the grannom, grass moth, and even some of the smaller beetles.

It is possible that the value of the palmer dressing in creating the impression of other insects can be seen in the Shadow Mayfly (page 55) and the Threlfall (page 93).

Sparkle Dun

This is an American no-hackle fly which suggests an emerger or a stillborn dun - a fly which has not been able to struggle free from the integument of the nymph.

Craig Mathews and John Juracek noticed great numbers of stillborns coming down with the hatching duns on a river in Montana. The nymphal shucks still attached to the body of the fly trapping its legs, 'sparkled and shimmered in the light.' [13]

The Sparkle Dun copied the imprint of the stillborn body lying in the surface film, no legs, no hackle, and a wing visible at the entry to the trout's window.

The Dry Fly

Hook: 16 to 20 for most of the small ephemeral flies.
Tying thread: to match the body colour.
Wing: the length of the wing should equal the length of the hook shank. The wing, deer hair dyed dun colour, should be tied in on the hook shank with the tips of the hair extending over the hook eye. The wing is then forced into an upright position by pulling it up and wrapping tying thread in front of the base, forcing the wing to stand upright. Once upright then continue to tie in the shuck at the tail.
Tail or shuck: sparkle poly yarn, or Z-lon (pronounced zeelon) tied in at the tail extending one half to a full hook shank length beyond the tail.
Body: finally, tie in a body of natural rabbit or synthetic dubbing dyed various shades of olive or brown, tapered from the tail to a slightly thicker body by the wing.

The deer hair wing, under pressure at the base, should flare out well on both sides.

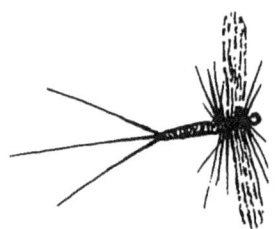

SPARKLE SPINNER

Designed by Craig Mathews and John Juracek of West Yellowstone this impressionist fly makes use of sparkle-poly yarn for the wing. This follows up an idea put forward by Vincent Marinaro. He said that he thought fresh mayfly spinners attracted the trout because of air bubbles trapped under the wings. Apparently sparkle-poly winged spinners have more strength and resist being bent back along the body as a standard wing will do. These, says Craig Mathews, outfish normal spinners in nearly all instances.

Hook: 12-20.
Thread: to match body colour.
Tail: start the tying by attaching dun fibres or synthetic microfibetts.
Wings: after tying in the tail tie in white sparkle-poly or Z-lon as flat wings.
Body: use natural or synthetic dubbings. The important colours in America are rusty, tan and olive. At home one might add orange.

SUPER GRIZZLY EMERGER

This is a variation, by John Goddard, of the Sparkle Dun. Craig Mathews and John Juracek of Blue Ribbon Flies in West Yellowstone noticed large numbers of stillborn duns on one of their rivers, duns which had been trapped and died because they had been unable to free themselves from the nymphal shuck which was still attached to their bodies. This partly empty shuck glistened in the light.

John Goddard noticed the same thing on his stretch of the Kennet, and designed a variation, after several years of experiments, which also has a sparkling tail to suggest the shuck. He says that from late June onwards when the small olives are hatching on the Kennet this new fly, which he calls the Super Grizzly Emerger, has been 'fantastically successful'.

The Dry Fly

Hook: Partridge Arrow Point size 18.
Tying silk: fine nymph, brown or purple.
Tail: silver or gold Krystal Flash, half a dozen strands three quarters of the length of the body.
Body: fluorescent orange Antron fibre supplied by Gordon Griffiths.
Wing: one red and one grizzle hackle (short in the flew) tied together.

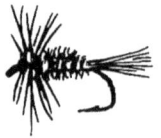

Terry's Terror

Dr Cecil Terry of Bath was one of the rods on the Hungerford water of the Kennet who were influenced by Harding, and Terry's favourite fly did not suggest anything in particular but stood in for quite a number of duns and emergers. Inevitably it became Terry's Terror, as inevitably as Greenwell became a Glory - alliteration has a compulsive charm - and this must have helped to spread its fame. Some of the Kennet rods hardly used anything else though nobody was certain what it was supposed to represent. However, like McCaskie's Green Cat, which was also something of a mystery, Terry's Terror got results.

Hook: 14, 16.
Tag: a short stub of orange and yellow goat hair, not mixed, one colour on one side, one on the other.
Body: a single strand of peacock herl, ribbed with flat copper or flat gold tinsel.
Hackle: red cock, not too bright a red.

The Impressionists

Tying silk: yellow gossamer.

One suspects that the tag was intended to imitate the shuck of a nymph which was still partly attached to the body of the fly.

The Threlfall

Richard Threlfall was a one-fly man. He fished only one pattern of a dry fly wherever he went - Itchen, Lambourn, Teme, Vyrnwy, the Yorkshire becks, Blagdon, and the great lakes of Ireland and Scotland - just one kind of a dry fly, a palmer hackle.

Why did he do this? 'Because,' he said 'I get no pleasure in stopping fishing and tying on one pattern of fly after another just because a fish is choosy'. So he chose one fly and only one fly to fish with. It would be one that had a wide appeal to the trout, would be well visible to the fisherman, should not get soft or waterlogged or difficult to dry. He went on:

> These conditions can only be met, I think, by a hackled fly, palmered well down the hook with plenty of stiff feather and in colour reddish or black. The hackles at the eye end of the hook should stick out straight or even forward, for if they start by sloping backwards they will soon slope too much.
>
> I have come to regard the body as unnecessary, since, unless an insect has a body of an unusual or vivid colour, such as the green midge, I am of opinion that the trout's attention to a fly on the surface comes almost wholly from the dimples made by its legs.

The Dry Fly

Anybody can satisfy himself how very noticeable to the fish's eye such dimples must be if he visits an aquarium where he can look up to the surface and observe the breaks in it made by small flotsam. As for the body of a fly, the body of a really buoyant fly never, or rarely, touches the surface.[14]

The fly was the simplest possible fly, it was not even a Bi-visible.

Hook: 10-18.
Body: a reddish or a black hackle palmered from eye to bend, making sure that the hackle at the head of the fly slopes forward and not towards the bend.

Howard Marshall, who watched Threlfall fish on the Lambourn, said that he had the great merit of casting accurately and very delicately. If a fish refused him and the fly had fallen correctly he would try once or twice more and if there was no response he would move on upstream and look for another rise. Marshall said that he knew many a man on the chalkstreams who fished one pattern of fly throughout the season and 'Threlfall caught as many trout in all conditions as the next man, and decidedly more than most of us'.[15]

Upside-Down Flies

John Goddard and Brian Clarke introduced the upside-down fly in their important study of trout and trout behaviour *The Trout and the Fly*[16] first published in 1980. It introduced fishermen to the trout's world with some remarkable underwater photography. For the first time we could see what men looked like to the fish and what the flies floating on the surface of the water looked like to the trout waiting for its food brought to it by the stream. Goddard and Clarke's researches convinced them that the standard conventional fly was all too frequently ignored by experienced fish, the fish that 'had seen it all before'.

Their answer was to tie a new kind of artificial dry fly, one that would not create uncertainty and alarm for the watching trout.

> We believe that with such a fish everything has to be right, including the body colour... When the experienced trout sees the fly floating towards him it sees the indentations of the feet and begins to rise upwards to intercept. But not for him a mad impulsive rush; he drifts up slowly and purposefully, in such a way as the fly, as he ascends, moves steadily from the mirror into his window. The wings begin to flare, and then join up with the abdomen of the fly on the very edge of window...
>
> In the normal course of events the artificial fly would move quickly across the rim of the window and would darken swiftly into a silhouette against the light above. *But the wary experienced fish does not allow it to do so...* the experienced fish rises until the fly is on the edge of the window and can be seen in full colour. Then the trout drops downstream with the fly, holding it there until he is satisfied that it is exactly what he wants. More commonly (it is why he has survived so long and has become an experienced fish) he will not.

So Goddard and Clarke designed a fly that would give the trout everything it wanted: a body, in the case of the dun, which stands aloft from the surface film, a body in the case of the spinner which lies in the surface film, feet indentations in the mirror, wings

The Dry Fly

to flare over the edge of the window; appropriate colouration, accurate profile in the window, and matching size.

They have taken many fish with flies that meet these requirements. They do do not think that the hook is a great deterrent to the trout. On the whole they find that these new upside-down dressings have taken many difficult fish.

> They are not infallible, any more than any artificial fly is infallible (indeed if an infallible fly were to be developed millions would leave the sport after half a dozen outings; and the fish would go with them). The new dressings are however a *supplement,* presenting the angler with a number of advantages over the conventional fly, when those advantages are most sorely needed: when he is confronted with difficult, experienced, desirable, and often *large* trout that turn up their imperious noses at wound-hackle flies.

The dressings of the upside-down flies given in *The Trout and the Fly* in 1980 have been improved and simplified by experiments over the years. Here is a typical new dressing known as the USD Para-Dun, the upside-down parachute dun:

> **Hook sizes:** varied according to the insect on the water.
> **Tying silk:** brown.
> **Tails:** now formed from a synthetic material, microfibetts, tied in well splayed and slightly round the bend of the hook.
> **Body:** this can be varied according to the species being represented: olive seal's fur substitute for the large dark and medium olive; a mix of olive and orange fur to represent the blue-winged olive; natural grey heron herl for the small dark olives; straw coloured fur to represent the pale wateries.
> **Wings:** calf tail dyed grey tied in sloping forward over the eye in a V-shape. Then the fly is taken out of the vice and turned upside down to receive the parachute hackle.

The Impressionists

Hackle: secure with a figure of eight a short V-shaped piece of stainless steel wire 1/50th of an inch in diameter round which the hackle is wound: olive for most of the olives, rusty dun for the pale watery and the blue-winged olive.

Goddard tells me that having specified these colours, most of the time he tends to carry several different sizes with grey bodies as this is without doubt the best pattern to use as a general pattern to represent most species of dun.

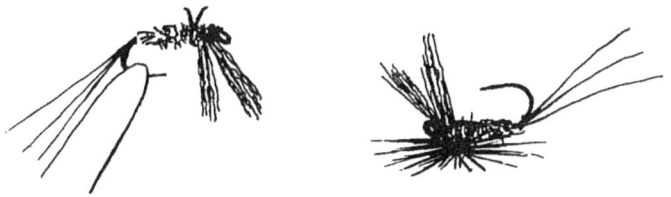

The sketch (left) shows the little V-shaped wire round which the hackle is wound parachute style; and (right) the completed upside down fly.

There have been earlier attempts at producing upside down flies. The first I am aware of, by Colonel Robert Venables (c.1612–1687), was simply to clip the hackles on the top of the fly.

> ...if I turn the feathers round the hook then I clip away those that are on the back of the hook, that so, if it be possible, the point of the hook may be forced by the feathers left on the inside of the hook to swim upwards...[17]

There were reports that upside-down flies were tied about 1910 but I have no confirmation. However these may have been the flies mentioned briefly in a book by Joscelyn Lane published (undated) by Seeley Service in London. From the text the likelihood is that it was published at some time in the late 1950s. Lane is irritatingly vague on the subject, merely summarising an article by a friend, known only as James, who gave some details of an upside down fly in an undated issue of *The Flyfishers' Journal*, which apparently, for the first time, used a parachute hackle. Lane merely says the hackle 'is tied flat to follow the general direction of the legs of the insect'. There is no explanation how this hackle was tied on.

WYLYE TERROR

One of many good patterns that suggest a number of olive duns. The tying is 'highly recommended by Frederick Mold who fished the upper river at Longbridge Deverill and has stood the test of time to this day.[18]

Clearly it was tied as an impressionist fly, making use of the long tail of a number of fibres to lift the body and the hook clear of the water.

Hook: 14.
Tail: honey dun cock hackle fibres longer than the length of the hook.
Body: undyed peacock quill.
Hackles: a mix of a shoulder hackle of honey dun cock and a head hackle of a light blue cock.

THE IMPRESSIONISTS

Footnotes to Chapter 3 The Impressionists

1. Paul Schullery *American Fly Fishing*, Nick Lyons Books, 1987.
2. See Abbotts Barton Survey in the Appendix page 109.
3. From an article in *Masters of the Dry Fly*, edited by J. Michael Migel, 1977.
4. Courtney Williams, *A Dictionary of Trout Flies*, A&C Black, 4th edition 1965.
5. Neil Patterson, *Chalkstream Chronicle*, Merlin Unwin Books, 1995.
6. F.M. Halford, *Dry Fly Entomology*, 1903.
7. F.M. Halford, *Dry Fly Fishing in Theory and Practice, 1889.*
8. David Jacques, *Fisherman's Fly and other studies*, A&C Black, 1965.
9. *Concise Oxford Dictionary of English Place Names*, OUP, 4th edition 1960.
10. Janus was a Roman God who faces two ways, so the Janus fly could also face two ways. It could be a Black Gnat or a Blue-winged Olive.
11. Mathews & Juracek, *Fly Patterns of Yellowstone*, Blue Ribbon Flies, 1987.
12. Datus C. Proper, *What the Trout Said*, Knopf, New York, 1982.
13. *Fly Patterns of Yellowstone - see above.*
14. *On a Gentle Art*, Richard Threlfall, Country Life, 1951.
15. Howard Marshall, *Reflections on a River*.
16. John Goddard and Brian Clarke, *The Trout and the Fly*.
17. Robert Venables, *The Experienced Angler*.
18. From an article by Steven Kemp in the summer number of *The Flyfishers' Journal*,1995. Frederick Mold wrote *Presenting the Fly to the Trout*published by Herbert Jenkins, 1967.

4. Six of the Best

Some of the best fishermen who have ever lived have not needed more than half a dozen flies.

Arthur Ransome, *Rod and Line*

Most of us carry far too many flies. If we are honest with ourselves we know perfectly well that we are never going to use all of them or even half. Most are there to be admired, as a coin collector admires his golden sovereigns and doubloons and an historian his shelves of rare editions. We collect our flies with the same enthusiasm and the same delight, and not a little surprise that without knowing it and without much effort we have acquired box-fulls.

Six of the Best

The other day I counted the number of flies in one of my dry flyboxes and it came, to my astonishment, to a hundred and twenty, and practically all of them had not been used, so far as I could remember, for many years. Some I had given to me, many I had tied, a few had been bought from tackle shops for reasons that I have long forgotten, and others had been bought on impulse at rummage sales at my club. Not that I would now wish to part with any of them, such beautiful little creatures, so delicate, so cunningly contrived, such miniature works of art. Many of them were at one time enormously fashionable for there are fashions in flies as there are in ladies' hats. Many years ago one could never go anywhere on the Itchen without a Beacon Beige, and indeed it was so popular that someone, I forget who, invented a ruthless rhyme about it which began

The Beacon Beige
Is all the reige

...and continued less successfully for several verses which fortunately I am now not able to recall. However, the point is that if you look at the records of the Abbotts Barton fishery of the Itchen (page 108) you will see that of the 859 trout caught in 1994 only seven were taken on a Beacon Beige - less than one percent - whereas the most popular fly was the Adams which took 85 trout or almost ten per cent of the total catch. Not that we can draw firm conclusions from all these statistical records, invaluable though they are; for we must remember that the more a particular fly is on the water and the more it is used by more and more members the more likely it is that it will become top of the list of successful patterns. When I fished that historic water of the Itchen in the 1950s I am almost certain that the Beacon Beige would have been the top fly while the Adams (page 24) had still to cross the Atlantic.

To sum up, with due regard to the fashions in flies and the invention of new designs that are more successful in persuading

The Dry Fly

the trout to the take, is it now possible to make a provisional list of flies that constitute a reliable, versatile half dozen or so - the figure imprints, especially the Grey Wulff. Even so, for the last four or five years when I have been on the river when *Ephemera danica* is hatching I have used nothing else but the Shadow Mayfly (page 55) with reasonable success; so the Shadow Mayfly it has to be, though it was a hard decision.

So now we have three patterns for the olives and one for the big mayfly which makes four with two to go. We must have at least one pattern for the sedge and here the Goddard Caddis (page 80) must lead the field. It was originally called the G&H Sedge - probably still is - because the original design was shared between Goddard and his friend Cliff Henry.

The five essential patterns so far are: the Adams; the Parachute Fly, preferably the Adams Parachute; the Funneldun; the Shadow Mayfly and the Goddard Caddis. What next? We have to find a fly which gives a good imprint of large and small black flies, such as the hawthorn (large) the black gnat (more or less medium) and the reed smut (rather small). You are probably going to suggest large, medium and small black hackles? You are quite right. It would do excellently on hooks 14, 18 and 20. All the same, may I choose another pattern - the Threlfall (page 93) - purely because of the hackle? Black hackles with reddish brown hackle points - sometimes known as Cochy Bonddhu hackles - are generally of better quality than all-black hackles. If you have got a good springy black hackle, that would do fine, but on balance I would prefer a blackish red and brown hackle of the first quality.

So now we have the six: Adams, Parachute Adams, Funneldun, Shadow Mayfly, and Threlfall, in different sizes. May I now go one over the six? I can't help it. I couldn't possibly leave it out and feel comfortable about it. It is an American pattern, a fairly large American pattern called the Humpy (page 43). Nobody knows what it is supposed to be. It has a remarkably good imprint but what does the imprint suggest to the trout? I have not the least idea. I have had various suggestions - a beetle, a cockchafer, a frog, among which was so arbitrarily fixed by Arthur Ransome in one of his essays in *Rod and Line*?

Certainly it is possible to fish with only half a dozen flies. To quote again the case of the Adams, not only does the Adams represent an olive dun of a particular kind but 'can suggest practically all the mayflies, olives, iron blues, blue-winged olives and pale wateries' (page 24). The Adams is not alone in this. Other new 'designer' flies have the same quality of being able to suggest quite a number of variations of the same species according to what the trout sees of them. So, let us make the attempt.

For the olive duns clearly we must start with the Adams. It floats high and suggests most if not all the olives we are likely to meet. Another new design which is invaluable when olives are on the water is the Parachute Adams. This, I must emphasise, is most likely to be a hatching olive nymph, a nymph that has just pulled itself out of the shuck and is preparing for take-off. It lies and rests on the surface film in the same way that a Gold-Ribbed Hare's Ear lies and rests on the surface film. The GRHE makes a good imprint but I would prefer the parachute design for its hackling.

If I may be allowed a third pattern I would go for the Funneldun (page 35). I have not used this pattern myself but it seems to me to meet all the requirements of the trout's vision and can represent all the olives.

So, there we are: three fly patterns for all the olive duns, we have, however, a problem with the spinner. Some say that the Parachute fly can double as the spinner because the close hackling could possibly give an imprint of wings. This may well be so and as I'm going to be tight-pressed to get all my flies into the half dozen I will leave a spinner for now. I have the great advantage in doing so as I rarely fish the evening rise these days. That may be a help.

The Dry Fly

I can only spare one pattern for the big mayfly which is a nuisance as there are at least four and probably five with excellent them - but I am not at all convinced that any of these is right. It may be pure superstition on my pail but I think the Humpy has a certain magic about it, a sleight of fly, which convinces the trout that whatever it is it is essential to have it. It took large fish in America when there was no hatch.

On the Test there was no fly on the water, but a Humpy cast at random brought up a monster. On a Devon lake - and again there was no hatch of fly - the Humpy, fished dry, cast out and allowed to drift with the wind brought up three good trout in under an hour and a half when nobody else was catching a thing. Magic it was. Indeed magic. It is true that it may work for me and for nobody else. I can't help it. I have an inexplicable reverence for the Humpy and I must have it in my box as - in cricketing terms - longstop, a deep cover point.

That's the whole point about flies: we develop a deep attachment to one particular design and it is, illogically, impossible to do without it. The choice of fly - and there are some 60 in this book - is very much a personal matter, as one might prefer roast duck to steak and kidney, but the next day hanker after the steak pie. With the choice of some 60 patterns of flies a mathematician would tell you that there are at least several hundred ways of using them, and if one is not too particular then perhaps several thousand. A Janus (page 104) is ideal for a black gnat in size 20 but if you want to use it for the blue-winged olive or the pale watery then you tie it on 14s or 16s. You can do many things like that. The Goddard Mayfly tied several sizes too small becomes one of the olives. A Parachute Adams can be turned into a sedge.

The reason why the new flies are so flexible is that it is no longer necessary to have a good model or copy of the natural insect. All that is necessary is to have a design that makes a good imprint on the water. In some cases there may be no need even to consider the use of wings. Colonel Harding again:

Six of the Best

We are inclined to picture the trout as lying at the apex of his cone, watching, like a spider in its web, for what may come on the surface. I doubt whether this is always a true picture. The trout can usually see the light pattern, the imprint of a floating fly, some time before it gets into the area of its window, and he probably starts at once to move towards the surface. In doing so he keeps on diminishing the area of his window, so that quite possibly the fly never managed to reach the area of his window: the trout's great maw sucks it down before that happens.

This cannot be proved until we have much greater underwater perception but it does seem a sensible picture of what sometimes may happen; and we have confirmation of this by the way in which a Threlfall or a Black Hackle are so effective in spite of the lack of wings.

We now at least can understand why 'the one-fly man' can do as well and sometimes better than the traditional way of fishing with the Halford pattern flies (see Howard Marshall's comments on page 94). In fact the new design of flies since Halford is the great achievement of our generation. We have broken free of the need to make models of insects and instead concentrate on the imprint or light pattern a fly makes on the surface of the water. We are in this way pointing to the developments of new designs in the coming century which at the moment we are unable to imagine. It is conceivable, for example that the use of feather for wings may be replaced by new and possibly as yet undiscovered synthetics. Who can say? Just as Cotton's flies were replaced after 70-odd years by the Bowlkers, and those flies by the inventiveness of the Victorians, so too our new flies of this century will almost certainly be displaced by those of a hundred years to come. We take part in a pattern of development which leads into the unknown and the flies which our generation have discovered must now be left to the legacy of time.

BIBLIOGRAPHY

Deane, Peter. *Peter Deane's Fly Tying,* Batsford, 1993
Dunne, J.W. *Sunshine & the Diy Fly,* A&C Black, 1924, 2nd ed. 1950
Edmonds and Lee. *Brook and River Trouting,* privately printed, 1916
Foster, David. *The Scientific Angler,* 1882
Goddard, John, and Brian Clarke. *The Trout and the Fly: a new approach,* Benn, 1980
Goddard, John.
    Trout Fly Recognition, A&C Black, 1966
    Fly Fishing Techniques, A&C Black, 1996
    John Goddard's Waterside Guide, Unwin Hyman, 1988
Greene, H. Plunket *Where the Bright Waters Meet,* 1924
Halford, F. M. *Floating Flies and How to Dress Them,* 1886
    Dry Fly Fishing in Theory and Practice, 1895
    The Modern Development of the Dry Fly, 1910
    The Dry Fly Mari's Handbook, 1913
Hall, John Inglis.
    Fishing a Highland Stream, Putnam, 1960, Viking 1987
Harding, Colonel E.W.
    The Flyfisher and the Trout's Point of View, Seeley Service, 1931
Harris, J.R. *An Angler's Entomology,* Collins, 952
Hills, John Waller.
    A History of Fly Fishing for Trout, Allen, 1921
    A Summer on the Test, Allen, 1924 and Deutsch 1983
Ivens, T.C. *Still Water Fly Fishing,* Deutsch, 1961
Jacques, David. *Fisherman's Fly,* A&C Black, 1965
Jorgensen, Poul, *see* Migel
Lane, Joscelyn. *Lake and Loch Fishing,* Seeley Service, 1954
Lapsley, Peter. *River Trout Fly Fishing,* Unwin Hyman, 1988
Lawrie, W.H. *A Reference Book of English Trout Flies,* Pelham, 1967
Lee, Art. *Fishing Dry Flies for Trout,* Atheneum, New York, 1982
Leeson, Ted. *The Habit of Rivers,* Lyons & Burford, New York, and Merlin Unwin Books, Ludlow, both 1994

THE DRY FLY

Marinaro, Vincent.
 A Modern Dry Fly Code, Putnam, New York, 1950
 In the Ring of the Rise, Lyons & Burford, New York, 1976
Marshall, Howard. *Reflections on a River,* Witherby, 1967
Mathews, Craig, and Juracek, John. *Fly Patterns of Yellowstone,* Blue Ribbon Flies, West Yellowstone, Montana, USA, 1987
Magee, Leslie.
 Fly Fishing, The North Country Tradition, Smith Settle, 1994
Migel, J. Michael (ed.), *Masters of the Dry Fly,* Lippincott, 1977, an anthology containing essay by Poul Jorgensen
Mottram, J.C. *Fly Fishing, Some New Arts and Mysteries,* The Field, c. 1915/16
O'Reilly, Pat. *Tactical Fly Fishing,* Crowood, 1990
O'Reilly, Peter.
 Trout & Salmon Rivers of Ireland, Merlin Unwin Books, 1991
Overfield, Donald.
 G.E.M. Skues, The Way of a Man with a Trout, Benn, 1977
Patterson, Neil. *Chalkstream Chronicle,* Merlin Unwin Books, 1995
Proper, Datus C. *What the Trout Said,* Knopf, New York, 1982
Pullman, G.P.R. *Vade Mecum of Fly Fishing for Trout,* 1841
Ransome, Arthur. *Mainly About Fishing,* A&C Black, 1959
 Rod and Line, Cape, 1929, O.U.P, 1980
Sandison, Bruce. *Trout Lochs of Scotland,* Unwin Hyman, 1983 Skues, G.E.M. *Minor Tactics of the Chalk Stream,* 1910
 The Way of the Trout with a Fly, 1921
Schullery, Paul.
 American Fly Fishing, Nick Lyons Books, New York, 1987
Stewart, W.C. *The Practical Angler,* 1857
Threlfall, Richard. *On a Gentle Art,* Country Life, 1951
Venables, Robert. *The Experienced Angler,* Antrobus Press,1969
West, Leonard. *The Natural Trout Fly and its Imitation,* Potter, 1921
Williams, Courtney.
 A Dictionary of Trout Flies, 4th ed, A&C Black, 1965
Wulff, Lee, *Lee Wulff on Trout Flies,* Stackpole, Harrisburg, 1980
 The Complete Lee Wulff, John Merwyn (ed.), Truman Tally Books, New York, 1989

APPENDIX

Successful Itchen Flies

Roy Darlington carried out an analysis of the successful fly patterns for the 1994 season at the Abbotts Barton fishery of the Itchen. The Adams comes first, followed by the Greenwell and Skues' Little Red Sedge.

Pattern	Trout Caught	% of Total
Adams	85	9.9%
Adams Parachute	2	0.233%
Alder	1	0.116%
B.W.O	15	1.75%
Beacon Beige	7	0.81%
Black Gnat	30	3.5%
Black Sedge	3	0.35%
Brown Sedge	6	0.7%
C.D.C Emerger	14	1.63%
C.D.C Orange Spinner	1	0.116%
Caperer	14	1.63%
Cinnamon Sedge	3	0.35%
Coachman	3	0.35%
Cree Duster	1	0.116%
Dark Olive	1	0.116%
Dark Nonedescript	2	0.233%
Emerger Nymph	2	0.233%
Funnel Dun Sedge	1	0.116%
G.R.H.E	29	3.38%
G.R.H.E Nymph	12	1.4%
Ginger Quill	4	0.466%
Goddard Sedge	4	0.466%
Greenwell's Glory	57	6.63%
Grey Buzzer	1	0.116%
Grey C.D.C	22	2.56%
Grey Wulff	32	3.725%
Hare's Ear	5	0.562%
Hare's Ear C.D.C	2	0.233%
Hawthorn	29	3.38%
Houghton Ruby	2	0.233%
Humpy	24	2.794%
Iron Blue Dun	10	1.16%
Iron Blue Emerger	4	0.466%
Irresistable	2	0.233%
Kite's Imperial	16	1.86%

The Dry Fly

Large Brown Hackle	13	1.51%
Little Deerhair Sedge	2	0.233%
Little Red Sedge	49	5.7%
Lunn's Particular	10	1.16%
Mayfly	30	3.5%
Medium Olive	5	0.562%
Morris Special	2	0.233%
Nonedescript	4	0.466%
Nymph	21	2.445%
Olive	2	0.233%
Olive Buzzer	2	0.233%
Olive C.D.C	17	1.98%
Olive Dun	5	0.582%
Olive Emerger	24	2.794%
Olive Nymph	2	0.233%
Olive Umbrella	1	0.116%
Orange Quill	5	0.582%
P.T. Nymph	4	0.466%
P.T.H.E Nymph	2	0.233%
Pale Watery Dun	1	0.116%
Para Hare's Ear	3	0.35
Parachute Dun	3	0.35%
Paradun	5	0.582%
Peacock Nymph	2	0.233%
Pheasant Tail	25	2.91%
Red Quill	4	0.466%
Red Spinner	4	0.466%
Red Wulff	14	1.63%
Royal Coachman	1	0.116%
Royal Wulff	3	0.35%
Sedge	48	5.59%
Shadow Mayfly	1	0.116%
Sherry Spinner	15	1.75%
Silver Sedge	11	1.28%
Small Brown Hackle	5	0.582%
Small Dark Olive	2	0.233%
Soldier Palmer	1	0.116%
Spent Mayfly	1	0.116%
The Telephone	1	0.116%
Thorax Olive Dun	17	1.98%
Tups Indispensable	44	5.122%
Wickham's Fancy	2	0.233%
TOTAL	859	

INDEX

Abbotts Barton 11; (River Itchen) 24, 101
Adams 75, 102, 103, 104
Adams Parachute 102
Adamson, J. 10
Aitken, George 10
Alder 6
Alice in Wonderland 12
Alston's Hackle 60
American Museum of Fly Fishing 54
Antron 75, 92

Bainbridge, George 1, 42
Barker, Thomas 55
Beacon Beige 101
Berls, Robert H. 10
Betts, John 10
Big Mayfly 53, 72
Bighorn Caddis 82
Bisland, W.E. 10
Bi-visible 26, 85
Black Drake 61
Black Duck 68
Black Gnat 6, 69
Black Hackle 26, 70, 72, 105
Black Sedge 86
Blacker, William 42
Blae & Black 68
Blagdon (lake) 7, 65, 93
Blagdon Blue Midge 69

Blue-Winged Olive 27, 42; Espersen's 31; dun 61; hatch 68
Blue Quill 45
Bolton Abbey Estate 10
Bossington Mill 5
Brabner, Nick 10
Bridgett, Anthony 10
Brown Upright 52
Brush, William A. 74
Burke, Jack 10

caddis flies 32
caenis 32
Campbell, Lt. Col. D.D. 10
Carroll, Lewis 12
Carshalton dodge 7
Caperer 84
Clarke, Brian 22, 66, 95
Clarke, Hugh 10, 21
Cochy Bonddhu 102
Cox, Willie 68
Cul de Canard 33

Daddy Longlegs 34
Dark Watchet 49
Darlington, Roy 10
Dashwood, Geoffrey 10
Davy, Sir Humphrey 1
Deane, Peter 10, 56

Debenham, Kim 51
Devine, Joe 10
Devon (lake) 104
Downs, Donald 10
Dunne, J.W. 8

Eady, Borlase 56
Edmonds & Lee, *Brook & River Trouting* 78
Elk Hair Caddis 85
Elphick, Brenda 69
emergers 65
Ephemera danica 54
Espersen, Morgens 10
  Espersen's BWO 31
Field, The 7, 8
Floating Flies & How to Dress Them 4, 6
Fly Fishing, Some New Arts & Mysteries 8
Flyfisher and the Trout's Point of View, The 11
Flyfishers' Club 4, 6, 10
Flyfishers' Journal 11, 70, 98

Fore & Aft Mayfly 61
Foster, David 1, 2, 3, 4, 9
Fox, Ken 69
Francis, Francis 1, 7
Funneldun 35, 37, 103

G&H Sedge 102
Ginger Quill 6
Grannom 6
Greene, Harry Plunket 45
Greene's Iron Blue 46

Greenwell, Canon 42
Greenwell's Glory 14, 41, 42, 77
Grey, Edward (later Viscount Grey of Falloden) 5, 65, 71
Grey Wulff 54, 102
Griffiths, Gordon 92
Goddard Caddis 102
Goddard, John 10, 17, 22, 57, 66, 80, 91, 94, 106
Goddard Mayfly 104
Goofus Bug 43
Gold-ribbed Hare's Ear 6, 14, 38, 50, 103;
  unwinged 39; winged 39, 40

Habit of Rivers, The 19
Halford, F.M. 3–6, 8, 9, 15, 40, 53, 79, 86
Halford's Rough Olive 50
Halliday, Leonard 24
Hammond of Winchester 72
Harding, Colonel E.W. 11–15, 17, 20–23, 41, 42, 55, 88, 104
Hare's Ear 19 Hare's Fleck 19
Hare's Lug 38
Hatching Lake Olive 50
Henry, Cliff 102
Herrington, Dr Godfrey 10
Hewitt, Ed 25
Hills, J. Waller 3, 5, 6, 52, 53, 73, 83
Holloway, Ron 10, 62
Hordern, 'Shrimp' 70
Horner Deer Hair 43
Houghton Club (River Test) 5, 53, 59, 83
Houghton Ruby 47

INDEX

Houghton Sedges 86
Humpy 43, 104
Hungerford Priory 56

Iron Blue 40, 45, 48, 72
Iron Blue Quill 45
Itchen, River 11, 30, 64, 71, 77, 94, 102
Iwerne Courtney (near Blandford) 12

Jacques, David 28, 61, 69
Janus 69
Jennings, Preston 54
Jorgensen, Poul 24
Juracek, John 89, 90, 91

Kemp, Steven 10
Kennet, River (Axford) 70; (Hungerford water) 16, 55, 92
Krystal Flash 92

Lake and Loch Fishing 88
Lambourn, River 73, 94
Lane, Joscelyn 49, 87, 97
Lane's Emerger 49
Lane's Sedges 87
Lapsley, Peter 29
Large Blue-winged Pale Watery 42
Large Dark Olive 64
Le Martre 65
Leckford 27, 51, 61
Leckford Olive Dun 50
Leeson, Ted 19
Limestone streams 7
Little Red Sedge 14, 81, 84
Loch Ordie 25

Lough Sheelin 68
Lough Arrow 7
Lunn, Alfred 53
Lunn, Mick 10, 51, 59, 86
Lunn, William 47, 52, 83
Lunn's Olive Dun 51
Lunn's Particular 52
Lyons, Nick 10

McCaskie's Green Cat 93
Mackie, Gordon 10
Marinaro, Vincent 10, 15, 16, 17, 40, 79, 90
Marryat, G.S. 3, 5, 6, 7, 8, 9, 53
Martin, Alex, (tackle shop) 74
Marshall, Howard 94
Marsh Court 28, 61
Mathews, Craig 10, 76, 80, 89, 90, 91
Matthews, EJ.T. 10, 75
Medium Olive Dun 64
Mick Lunn's Shaving Brush 59
Microfibetts, 96
microflies 62
Midge Emerger 66
midges 65
Modern Dry Fly Code, A 15
Mold, Frederick 98
Mole Fly 51
Mottram, Dr J.C. 8

Neversink River 25
No-hackle Fly 89
North Country wet fly patterns 23

Ogden of Cheltenham 1
Olive Spinner 64

Orange Partridge 72, 73
Orange Sedge 86
Orange Spinner 27, 28
Orange Quill 27, 72
O'Reilly, Pat 10
O'Reilly, Peter 10

pale wateries 51
Palethorpe, J. Arthur 56
palmer dressing 26
Palmer Sedge 85
Patterson, Neil 10, 35, 36, 66
Parachute Adams 75, 104
Parachute Fly 30, 74, 102-103
Peacock Fly 76
Pheasant Tail 46, 77
Piscatorial Club (Itchen) 77
Pollen, Major Hugh 10
Poly May Dun 57
Poult Bloa 78
Proper, Datus C. 85
Pulman of Axminster 1, 3

Red Quill 6, 72, 79
Reid, J. 10
River Keeper, The 53
Robinson, Guy 10, 27, 84
Robson, Kenneth 10

Sawyer, Frank 32
Schullery, Paul 24
Schultz, Dave 76
Scientific Angler, The 2
Sedge Fly 31, 72
    light patterns of the sedge 88
Seeley Service 88, 97

Shadow Mayfly 55, 102
Silver Sedge 6, 87
Skues, G.E.M. 6, 11, 12, 47, 49, 72,
    81, 84, 89; Skues' Caenis 33;
    Skues' Iron Blue 46, 47
Sparkle Dun 89, 91
Sparkle Poly Yam 90
Sparkle Spinner 91
Spent Olive 64
Spring Olive 64
Starr, Robert 10
Stewart of Edinburgh 1
Summer on the Test, A 83
Super Grizzly Emerger 91
Suspender Midge Pupa 66

Teme, River 93
Terry, Dr Cecil 56, 92
Test, River 5, 60, 62, 65
    (at Chilbolton) 30; (Leckford
    Estate) 51 (Marsh Court) 61
Thorax Dun 15, 16
Thirlway, Hal 69
Threlfall, Richard 93, 94
Threlfall (the fly) 77, 85, 93, 94, 102,
    105
Todd, Helen 74 Troth, A1 85
Trout and the Fly, The 22, 96

upside-down flies 96, 97
USD Para-dun 96

*Vade Mecum of Fly Fishing for Trout,
    The* 3
Valentine, Tom 10
Venables, Colonel Robert 97

INDEX

Vyrnwy, Lake 93

Wagner, Colton 10
Walton, Izaak 55
Wandle, River 7
Ward, Dr 14
Wellington, Herb 10, 75
Weir Wood 34
Where the Bright Waters Meet 45
Wilderness, The (River Kennet) 22
Williams, Courtney 79
Willis, A. 10
Winchester School 2
Wright, James 42
Wulff, Lee 53
Wylye Terror, 98

Yellowstone, West 76
Yorkshire becks, 72, 93

Z-lon 90

PLATE A

Sparkle Dun Duck Fly Blagdon Green Midge
Caperer Black Gnat Beacon Beige
Gold-ribbed Hare's Ear Micro Orange Quill
Upside-down Dun Adams
Threlfall
Brown Upright Houghton Ruby

PLATE B

Shadow Mayfly Alston's Hackle Mayfly
Poly May Dun
Grey Wulff Poly May Spinner

PLATE C

Silver Sedge   Houghton Black Sedge   Terry's Terror
Elk Hair Caddis   Houghton Orange Sedge   Winged Caperer
Little Red Sedge   Humpy
Palmer Sedge   G&H Sedge

PLATE D

Winged GRHE   Suspender Midge   Iron Blue Dun
Super Grizzly Emerger   Greenwell's Glory   Lunn's Particular
Leckford Olive Dun   Blue-winged Olive   Lunn's Olive Dun
Dark Watchet   Orange Spinner   Pheasant Tail
Last Hope
Parachute Fly   Funneldun   Janus

Also published by Merlin Unwin Books
www.merlinunwin.co.uk

CHALK AND CHEESE Charles Hamer
THE HEALING STREAM Laurence Catlow
ONCE A FLYFISHER Laurence Catlow
THAT STRANGE ALCHEMY Laurence Catlow
HOW TO FLYFISH John Symonds
FLYCASTING SKILLS John Symonds
POCKET GUIDE TO MATCHING THE HATCH Lapsley & Bennett
POCKET GUIDE TO FISHING KNOTS Peter Owen
COMPLETE ILLUSTRATED DIRECTORY OF SALMON FLIES Chris Mann
TROUT FROM A BOAT Dennis Moss
NYMPHING: THE NEW WAY Jonathan White
THE FEATHER BENDER'S FLYTYING TECHNIQUES Barry Ord Clarke
TYING FLIES WITH CDC Leon Links
SONG OF THE SOLITARY BASS FISHER James Batty
GT: A FLYFISHER'S GUIDE TO GIANT TREVALLY Peter McLeod
FISHING WITH HARRY Tony Baws
THE FISHERMAN'S BEDSIDE BOOK BB
CONFESSIONS OF A CARP FISHER BB
FLYFISHING FOR COARSE FISH Dominic Garnett
CANAL FISHING Dominic Garnett
HOOKED ON LURE FISHING Dominic Garnett
FISHING WITH EMMA David Overland
GET FISHING Allan Sefton
SECRET CARP Chris Yates
FALLING IN AGAIN Chris Yates

www.ingramcontent.com/pod-product-compliance
Lightning Source LLC
Chambersburg PA
CBHW040313170426
43195CB00020B/2959